BRUISED ...
BUT NOT BROKEN

The story of Eddie Murison
told by
Betty McKay

Christian Focus Publications

© 1994 Betty McKay and Eddie Murison
ISBN 1-85792-113-5
Reprinted 1998

Published by
Christian Focus Publications Ltd
Geanies House, Fearn, Ross-shire,
IV20 1TW, Scotland, Great Britain.

Printed and bound in Great Britain by
Caledonian International Book Manufacturing, Glasgow

Cover design by Donna Macleod

Contents

FOREWORD

I read once of a sculptor who had worked on a block of granite for a long time without much success. The granite was so hard that all his efforts resulted in removing small chips of stone from the block. A colleague came into his Studio one day and the conversation moved to the great block of hard rock. 'It is useless,' said the sculptor, 'I can make no impression on this block, it is much too hard, so I'll have to get rid of it.'

'Let me try,' said his friend. Eventually the block arrived at its new destination. The Artist began working on it .... At times he lost heart, and was about to give up, but there was something about the block which was a challenge to him. After a long time of shaping, chipping, smoothing and polishing, out of this hard, resisting granite block came the artist's *masterpiece*. The patience, care, workmanship and determined persistence of the artist had won in the end.

In my almost quarter of a century as a prison chaplain, I have met many men who remind me of that hard, unresponsive block of granite. Men whose evil past has made them hard, bitter, aggressive and irresponsible. At first they look like hopeless cases, where nothing and no one can make an impression

7

on their hardened lives. Yet the Heavenly Artist does
not give up, but continues to chip with the hammer
of love and the chisel of grace, until gradually the
change begins to come, and eventually out of the
marred and damaged mess begins to emerge one of
God's Masterpieces.

Eddie Murison's story is one which shows that
no matter how far a man goes down into the mire of
sin, addiction and depravity, the Heavenly Artist,
namely the Lord Jesus Christ, can begin to work on
that life. As in Eddie's case the material was hard and
at times like the Potter's Vessel in Jeremiah 18: 1-6;
he needed to be broken down again and have the
offending stone of rebellion, anger, irresponsibility
and sin taken away. But the Saviour does not want
his child to live like the 'wretched man' in Romans
7: 18-24, who has no victory in his life, or experience. So the Saviour keeps on chipping, shaping,
lifting and polishing his child until 'The law of the
Spirit of Life in Christ Jesus makes us free from the
bondage of sin and death.'

I am sure every reader of this story will continue
to pray for Eddie and Leslie, that our Heavenly Artist
will work on their lives and will make them vessels
that are sanctified and used to extend God's King-
dom.

Canon Noel Proctor MBE
Chaplain of HM Prison,
Manchester

'Christ will not deal roughly and rigorously with those that come to him, but will use all gentleness and tenderness to them; passing by their greatest sins, bearing with their present infirmities, cherishing and encouraging the smallest beginnings of grace, and comforting and healing wounded consciences.'
[Note in Cruden's Concordance - Alexander Cruden]

THE BRUISING

The sturdy three-year-old, clad in black dungarees and white polo-necked jumper, trotted along the city pavement hand-in-hand with his Uncle Jamesie. They weren't going far. Just a few streets away to another block of tenement houses.

Young Eddie was intent on one thing. He was going to his Mum. She had slipped out to see a friend, but he wanted her. That's why Uncle Jamesie was taking him to find her.

When they reached Spa Street Uncle Jamesie rapped on the door. Though it wasn't her own house, Eddie's Mum opened it. Then, before Eddie could say or do anything, he heard the rough tones of a man's voice coming from the room inside.

'Who is it?'

Eddie's Mum answered, more gently. 'It's little Eddie.'

'What's *he* want? We dinna want him here.'

Not many words, but the man's tone of voice was enough.

Memory becomes hazy at this point, blanked out by the searing pain of rejection.

The years that followed would confirm and reinforce that short, sharp lesson on the doorstep.

Eddie's whole life would be shaped by the terrible knowledge that he was a reject. Not wanted.

1

GRANDA

It was just before the New Year, 1958, and Granda had a fair few drinks inside him. The open fire had made the living-room very warm and Granda was stripped to the waist.

'Just like he is when he's going to fight,' thought Eddie, remembering times when he'd seen his Granda rip off his shirt in a rage and fling it down before tearing into the man who had crossed him, fists flying.

But Granda was sitting quietly just now, writing something. And then another man came down the stairs and into the room. And suddenly, out of nowhere, a fight was on. Tables went flying, and Granda threw a chair. Uncle Jamesie joined in, brandishing a poker.

Eddie was scared stiff. He ran to his Mum. 'Come on,' she said, lifting him into her arms. 'Let's get out of here 'til it quietens down a bit.' The neighbours wouldn't mind them going in next door for a while.

That was one of the good things about living in Froghall. Although it was in the centre of Aberdeen, the area around Froghall Avenue was a little com-

munity in itself. Everybody knew everybody else
and if they sometimes knew a bit *too* much, well at
least they wouldn't see you stuck for help.

The tall, granite blocks of tenements were owned
by the council and Granda lived on the middle floor
of number eighteen. Granda, Jim Murison, was
originally from Peterhead but when his wife died, he
and his eight surviving children - four boys and four
girls - had moved to the three bedroomed tenement
in Aberdeen.

Jim was one of the travelling folk - a man with a
sharp eye for a bargain, who knew how to handle
himself when it came to a fight. Which it often did,
for he loved a drink and the two things just seemed
to go together. Many a time in the carnivals and
travelling fairs, 'Spitty' Murison had challenged the
professional boxers - and won. The nickname 'Spitty'
came from his practice of spitting in the face of his
opponent before he hit him.

Ordinarily he managed to make a living by going
round the streets, knocking on doors, offering charms,
doing odd jobs or buying anything folk wanted to
sell. In the old days, when his father was alive,
they'd gone round with a horse and cart, but by the
time Eddie was born, Jim had acquired an old green
van and his own son Jamesie acted as driver. Jim, in
his old checked 'bonnet', did the 'sprachin' - the
actual doorstep bargaining.

Long practice had made him a master at that.
He'd buy anything - from scrap metal to antiques -

and he'd pit his wits against the owner to get the best price.

'Yer eye's yer merchant' was his private maxim, though it was never openly spelled out to his clients. Let them find out the hard way! 'What you see is what you're buying. If you canna see the problem, that's your tough luck. Nae comeback.'

Such bargaining was thirsty work, so Jim would call into a pub. Sometimes his pals would be there, and sometimes others who were not so fond of him. It was one of these who decided to have a joke at his expense one day.

Grabbing a pencil he wrote in bold letters: Jimmy Murison canna read. Whereupon the said Jimmy sprang up: 'I can read *that*!' he bellowed - and then splattered the guy right across the pub.

At home he was a strict man and did his best to see that none of his family got into trouble - with the law or in any other way. As a late teenager his daughter Muriel found some of his restrictions irksome - especially his ban on going out with boys. But, being her father's daughter, she found ways and means of her own.

Looking down from the first floor window and spotting one of her boyfriends lingering in the street below, she'd announce that something was amiss with the washing line and she'd better go and fix it. And so she would gain a few moments stolen freedom for a quick cuddle. Later on she must have managed a bit more than these illicit moments, for

she was barely out of her teens when Eddie made his
appearance.

Jim Murison's reaction is not recorded, but he
allowed his daughter to live on at home and from
then on he was 'Granda' to Eddie. The close bond
which sprang up between them in those first few
years lasted until the older man died.

But in those early years, tensions grew between
father and daughter. For Muriel had a new boyfriend
and Granda didn't like him. He was a 'scaldie', a
'flattie', both derogatory terms for anyone who was
not one of the travelling people. This new suitor
lived with his mother in Spa Street. When he came
visiting, Granda would take care to be out. Many a
time he advised his daughter to have nothing to do
with the lad. But she was as headstrong as he, and the
courtship continued. Besides, she argued, it would
be good for Eddie to have a father.

The trouble was that to this boyfriend, Eddie was
just a nuisance, an unwanted extra. He made no
effort to hide his feelings, as three year old Eddie
discovered the day his Uncle Jamesie took him
round to their doorstep ....

But the wedding went ahead anyway and Eddie
had to go and live in the Spa Street house, away from
his beloved Granda. Right from the start he hated the
fear-chilled atmosphere of his new home.

When Eddie was five he was sent to Spa Street
School. His new 'Granny' bought him a suit for the
occasion. To his horror he was dressed up in a smart

jacket, short trousers, shiny brown shoes and - the
greatest indignity - a green schoolcap!

Eddie was totally affronted. 'I'm no wearin'
this!' he protested to his mother. But it was no good.
He was marched off in his smart new clothes into the
huge forbidding building that was school.

Once inside he was instinctively wary and alert.
He was aware of highly polished floors and a long,
shiny white corridor. It was a totally alien world.
'What's going to happen to me here?' he wondered.

In fact he did not have to stay at that particular
school for very long for the family were to move to
Deanslock Terrace. Between the moves they stayed
for a while with Eddie's aunt Margaret and her son,
Eddie's cousin Dennis.

It was there that a whole series of disasters struck
Eddie. First it was his balloon. He'd been given a
lovely shiny red balloon, and somehow it got burst.
Then he became ill with a mixture of measles and
mumps and a cold on top of it all. But worse than that
was losing his rabbit. Eddie really loved his soft,
cuddly pet and when it died, he cried and cried,
refusing to be consoled. How could it have died
when he loved it so much, he wondered. Why? The
final straw came one day when his stepfather, Birch,
went to the local Timmermarket. This was an annual
event - a huge open market, originally for timber but
later extended to include all kinds of articles. This
day, Birch arrived home with a toy Luger pistol for
Eddie. Delighted with his unexpected gift, the wee

boy eagerly showed it to his cousin Dennis.

'Far's mines?' wailed Dennis. He made a grab for the gun and the battle was on. As the two boys scuffled about together, Birch burst into the room. Swearing and cursing he swept up all Eddie's toys and shoved them into a box and the two wee boys watched in amazement as he flung everything out to the dustbin.

He came back inside and thrust his angry face into Eddie's: 'If I canna gie you somethin' in peace, you're gettin' nothin'!'

Eddie was stunned. What had he done wrong? A bit of a fight with Dennis was nothing. His lip quivered. Why did things never go right? he thought miserably. First he'd lost his balloon, then his rabbit, and now all his toys. Why? Though he searched long for an answer, he found none.

Not long after this he and Dennis were coming home from school together when they were set upon by some bigger boys. The lads grabbed them and forced them into a semi-derelict old house. It was darkish inside, but Eddie could see the floorboards had all gone, leaving only wooden joists with a deep drop below. Before they knew what was happening Eddie and Dennis were blindfolded, thrust on to the joists and dared to walk across.

The older boys jeered and laughed as their terri-fied victims staggered across as best they could. Eddie felt the fear clutching at his stomach as he put one foot in front of the other. What if he fell? How

far down would it be? Would he be killed? Would
they leave him there?

Somehow both boys made it to the other side
safely while their tormentors ran away laughing.

Eddie's whole life seemed to be haunted by fear
in those early years. And underlying everything was
the fear of his stepfather, a fear which was slowly
hardening into hatred. Eddie felt rejection in his
every glance.

Nor was the man's resentment confined to glanc-
es - violence was never far below the surface. He
would pick on the least misdeed and punish Eddie,
and if his Mum butted in to help, she would get it too.
The angry man would pin his wife against a wall:
'That basket doesna' belong here!' he would shout.
And there would be blows, first for his wife and then
for Eddie.

One night when he was eight Eddie was sitting up
in bed in his orange and white striped pyjamas. He
still had the light on when Birch came in and started
making his usual nasty comments.

'I'll *get* you.' Eddie daren't say the words out
loud, but he thought them as hard as he could. And
as Birch turned to go out of the room, Eddie stuck out
his tongue and pulled the most horrible face he could
manage. Unfortunately Birch was just passing the
mirror and saw everything. The hiding Eddie got for
that hurt - he couldn't sit comfortably for about a
week - but it was worth it!

A short time later Birch got a job as gardener at

Skibo Castle and the family moved north. For Eddie this meant another new school, amongst complete strangers. He found it hard to settle, especially when the teacher made him stand in a corner for some minor misdeed. He felt such a fool. He decided to get his own back.

That weekend he broke into the school, went to his classroom and tore up all the jotters and exercise books he could find. Then he set fire to them. It was quite a blaze. In fact he began to get a bit worried so he grabbed the fire extinguisher and sprayed it around wildly, leaving tell-tale footprints in the foam!

When the damage was discovered on Monday morning, the police were called in and the 'prints' gave Eddie away. It was his first brush with the law!

This incident did nothing to ease the constant tension at home. Fear and anger and the constantly rubbed-in rejection grew like a cancer in nine-year-old Eddie. Inside he felt cold and hard. It was the only way he could cope with the daily jibes. Like the teatime when they were eating a pile of sandwiches. When it came to the last one on the plate, Birch said: 'That's mines. I'm the breadwinner in this hoose!'

Maybe it was this last straw that gave Eddie his idea. He waited for an opportunity and then got on his little bike and set off for Aberdeen and Granda.

It was quite a long way - about a hundred and forty miles - and by the time he got to Inverurie Eddie was completely lost. So why not ask a policeman?

'Are you running away?' the policeman enquired, kindly enough.

'No,' said Eddie. 'I'm just going to see my Granda.'

'Well come and have a cup of coffee first,' the policeman insisted. The lad followed meekly and a policewoman brought him coffee. Then she started asking questions. But something inside Eddie warned him, 'You don't tell these people anything'. Not even when they asked if he was running away because he was getting hidings at home.

'I'm nae tellin',' was all he would say. If Birch found out that he'd told the police, who knew what he might do to his Mum? Or him?

Eddie had to wait quite a while in Inverurie Police Station, but in the end things were sorted out and Granda sent Uncle Jamesie to collect him.

At last he was free from his stepfather. For a while anyway. He would enjoy living with Granda again.

Being back in Froghall Avenue was like being let out of jail! For starters, nobody grudged him food. In fact he could get a piece and jam any time he liked - even without asking! In his stepfather's house you had to ask for everything - and even then the answer would probably be 'No'. But Granda's house was completely different.

It was an open house. The kettle was never off and great pots of steaming soup filled the kitchen with a hungry-making aroma.

Eddie never knew what he'd find cluttering up the room when he came home from school - bits of cars or motorbikes, broken chairs or other furniture that needed mending. People were always coming to buy or sell things because Granda was wheeling and dealing in just about everything. No doubt about it, Granda was a special guy.

The house was just as busy at night because Granda loved music - Scottish music. He'd take out his old accordion, sit on a kitchen chair at the window and play for hours. There'd be music and drinking and singing and people crowding in to enjoy it all.

Sometimes Granda would tell stories - tales of the old days when the whole family would live outside for weeks at a time in tents and trailers.

'I'm nae goin' to ma bed. I want to hear more,' Eddie would think as more folk arrived and the stories went on. He loved to hear how Granda used to poach rabbits and roast them on an open fire and brew endless cups of 'slab' - the gypsies' word for tea.

One time a man had come while they were all sleeping, cut part of a tent and reached through and caught one of the wee girls by her hair, trying to steal her. When she screamed the man took off through the woods with Granda chasing him in nothing but his long johns!

'If I'd caught him, I'd ha' killed him,' Granda always ended. And Eddie believed him.

Granda always had time for Eddie. He taught him how to use his hands and make things with wood and metal. And he taught him how to fight. They'd go together into the small back bedroom and have boxing lessons. 'Come on - let's see what you're made of,' Granda would say. To Granda, being able to handle yourself in a fight was one of life's basic necessities. And he saw to it that Eddie learned that lesson well!

2

SCHOOL DAYS

By the time Eddie reached Old Aberdeen Secondary School he was known as a 'hard case'. Most lessons meant little or nothing to him - though he didn't mind practical subjects like woodwork - anything to do with his hands tied in with some of the things Granda had shown him, so he accepted these. But for most of the formal lessons he would just mentally switch off and refuse to co-operate.

Maths was one example. It was a complete mystery to Eddie. And he detested the particular teacher, sensing that the man hated having him in his class as much as Eddie hated being there. The teacher lost no opportunity to show his dislike or to belittle Eddie. So, when he should have been concentrating on calculations, Eddie would be inwardly uttering threats: 'I'm gonna punch this guy's lights oot. I'm gonna get him right on the chin.' And once or twice he came very near to doing it. One strong thought stopped him - the thought of what Granda would say. He knew that if he touched the teacher, Granda would have chinned *him*!

The only teachers Eddie allowed to get through to

him even slightly were the ones whom he felt showed a genuine interest in him as a person.

One of these was the gym teacher, Mr Spalding. Eddie enjoyed PT and was good at it, especially cross-country running. He sensed that Mr Spalding liked him as a person and even respected his ability. One day he asked Eddie to be part of a group representing the school at a big local area event.

'Ye hinna got the shoes, ye hinna got the shorts, I still want you in on Saturday. No excuses - OK?'

It was a blunt enough invitation, calculated to pre-empt any refusal and for once Eddie went along with it, secretly delighted that the teacher genuinely wanted him there and obviously looked on him as an asset.

A party of eight - four boys and four girls - travelled to the venue by minibus and Eddie came in a respectable seventeenth in a field of hundreds.

Spalding continued to encourage Eddie but stick-ability was not one of his characteristics. He didn't turn out on Saturday again. A more attractive option was to hang around street corners with the bigger lads.

The only times Eddie looked forward to at school were the break times. Then he could go out and do what he most enjoyed - fight. His early rejection made him ultra-sensitive to remarks the other boys made and he often took them the wrong way, delib-erately magnifying an innocent comment into a reason to lash out. His own inner hurt fuelled his desire to see others hurt in turn.

For a short time Eddie had a friend at school. He was a quiet guy called Andy. He didn't speak much, but there was something about him that Eddie felt he could relate to. Maybe it was the way they'd both been brought up. They spent a good bit of time together - until the set-up.

Following in Granda's footsteps, even at school Eddie had started 'dealing'. One day he had acquired a medal and was hoping to get five pounds for it. Andy knew about the deal and just when Eddie's 'client' was about to hand over the cash a group of bigger lads came round the corner and fell right on top of them. Eddie didn't get a chance.

It wasn't the sort of thing you could complain to the teachers about so there was nothing Eddie could do about his loss. Next day he found out that it was his 'mate' Andy who had tipped the older boys off and set him up, and another layer of hardness formed inside him as he resolved: 'I'm nae goin' to trust anybody ever again.' From now on it would be acquaintances only - not friends.

One day Eddie and a few other boys swaggered into school with shaved heads, Wrangler jeans, white shirts and braces, and calf length Doctor Marten boots. They had often been in trouble for tormenting other kids and this gear must have made them look even more threatening. The class teacher sent them all to the Headmaster.

As a punishment they were ordered to sit outside

the Head's office every break time until further
notice. Eddie had no intention of doing any such
thing. When break time came, he went home.

Next day when the Head challenged him about it,
Eddie told him straight. 'If I have to sit outside your
office for my play piece, then you can stick your
school. I'd rather sit at hame.'

After that Eddie pleased himself whether he
turned up to school or not. When he did appear he'd
go to the Head and tell him that he'd been off. 'I've
nae excuse,' he'd say. 'I just didna want to come to
school.'

For a while Eddie would get the belt for this
behaviour, but in the end the Head realised that the
belt was having no effect on Eddie. 'Awa' to yer
class,' he would say.

This reaction - an acceptance of facts as they were
- provoked a surprising response in Eddie. He decided to make the Head a gift - a picture in wood, using
various shades and shapes fitted together, as his
Granda had showed him.

When it was ready Eddie went to the Head's
office and, just as he was about to knock, he heard
voices. He recognised the tones of the Head and also
the Principal Officer. 'He's a hard case,' the Head
was saying. 'We're going to have trouble with him
later.'

A warm glow of pleasure spread through Eddie.
Maybe it was for the wrong reasons, but he was
being noticed. And it felt good!

The authorities didn't quite see him that way though, and a letter arrived home summoning a family adult to go to school with Eddie for an interview. Granda deputed Aunt Margaret to attend.

When they arrived, four boys were sitting in the Headmaster's office and they were allowed to state their complaints about the way Eddie bullied them.

Eddie and Aunt Margaret listened in silence. Then Aunt Margaret's eyes swept contemptuously along the row of boys before she finally spoke.

'Well, these four boys are all bigger than Eddie and if they canna handle a wee problem, there's nothing I'm gonna do aboot it.'

Then, fixing the Headmaster with an uncompromising look, she added: 'An' if you're the Headmaster and canna control them here, then that's *your* problem!'

And she swept out of the office with a triumphant Eddie in her wake. 'Oh yes!' he thought. 'Good for her - she gave it to 'em straight.'

But his moment of triumph was short-lived for, once outside, Aunt Margaret gave Eddie an almighty swipe. 'Don't you do that again!' she ordered. He knew he'd pushed her as far as she would go that time.

If school days were not the happiest days of his life, the nights were much more satisfactory to Eddie. He was free to roam around as he liked as long as he was in before eleven. Granda would sit and wait until his son Michael came in and once he was in, Granda would lock the door and go off to his bed, his household safely locked up for the night.

Or so he thought. But that was the time when Eddie would be ready for going out again. This time it was through the window and down the drainpipe. (Not for nothing was he good at PT!) He'd meet up with lads older than himself and roam the streets until two or three o'clock, returning via the drain-pipe.

Their main hang-out was a city centre graveyard. It was the era of the skinheads. Both boys and girls had their own gear and they'd sit around, looking out for guys with motorbikes. The boys wore Wrangler blue jeans and Dr Marten's brown calf length boots beneath black Crombie coats. Concealed beneath the coat collars was a clutch of penny fish-hooks intended to 'catch' any person unwise enough to grab them by the collar! They carried brollies - which doubled as swordlike weapons - and the whole outfit was topped by a bowler hat. The final touch of class was a red handkerchief worn in the top pocket, secured with a pearl pin. They would have other weapons also - chains, hammers, knives - and they'd be just itching to start a rumpus.

Eddie really enjoyed fighting with these gangs. Even though he was a few years younger than most of the guys, he loved the adrenaline-filled excite-ment of a good fight.

One night they moved off to the beach area where there was a carnival. Then suddenly a gang of

Glasgow motorbikers arrived and the fight was on.
When the Aberdeen lads realised they were outnum-
bered they ran into the carnival, twisting this way
and that, grabbing anything that came to hand. Eddie
knew it would be a big fight. He snatched a crossbow
from one of the stalls and aimed it right at one guy's
face. He was a lot bigger than Eddie, but fear gave
Eddie a kind of courage.

'If you come near me pal, I'm gonna give you this
right in the puss!' Then, without waiting to see,
Eddie fired. He missed - but the intent had been
there.

When no outsiders came, the different Aberdeen
gangs - the Skinheads, the Gringos, the Mastrick
mob - would fight each other. Eddie loved the
atmosphere ... lassies round about ... guys boasting
of what they'd done ... plenty of drink and maybe a
few bits of drugs. It was brilliant! For once in his life
he felt accepted - and he loved it. It was all he wanted.

Some nights they'd go really wild after a few
drinks and the gangs would tear up Union Street,
fling a hammer through a shop window and grab
what they wanted - a bottle of wine, jewellery,
whatever. The place would suddenly be full of
bobbies, but that all added to the sport. There was
little they could do in all the confusion of the gangs.
Such excitement was the breath of life to Eddie as a
young teenager.

In the midst of the melee Eddie instinctively acted
on one of Granda's maxims: 'Always make sure you

benefit out of everything you do.' So Eddie would grab whatever he could, thinking, 'I'm all right here.'

Besides, Eddie needed the extra 'goods' so he could get money to be able to run around with the bigger lads. You needed cash to get the right gear - and that was essential. And this was one way to get it.

Another was to 'persuade' other kids to 'give' him money. At school, Friday afternoons were scheduled for swimming, archery or other sports. But Eddie and his pals would slip off to the carnivals. There were always kids there from other schools and Eddie would 'talk' them into parting with their money - or anything else he fancied.

He didn't always get away with it for sometimes the Police would appear and there'd be a chase through the carnival - round the booths, under the whirling horses on the merry-go-round. Once he was caught and taken to Juvenile Court for mugging kids.

It didn't worry Eddie. He enjoyed the 'education' the older boys were giving him. There seemed to be no end to their 'pranks'.

Uncle Jamesie had taught him the rudiments of driving and one day he and another boy broke into a bakery, ate their fill of biscuits and drove a bakery van out onto the street. They didn't get far that time before they smashed into the back of a parked car, but two days later they tried again. This time they were bolder. They took a van loaded with baking and went round the streets, tooting the horn, selling the goods and pocketing the money. Their day was made when two policemen came and bought a couple of pies! The whole situation appealed to Eddie's sense of humour - that he could be driving a stolen van and selling stolen pies to cops!

He didn't get away with it for long of course - and there was some hiding when they finally caught him. It meant another trip to the Juvenile Court.

Not that these experiences deterred him. One New Year's day Eddie was short of money, so he broke into a shop and cleared £250 from the till. That night he went out for a few drinks with a pal. Suddenly Birch appeared in the pub. He tried to persuade Eddie to go home with him.

But Eddie had no intention of going with him so he ran out and off along the street into a tenement block. He ran up the stairs to the first landing - and immediately realised his mistake. There was no way he could get out and Birch was close behind.

Reaching into his pocket he pulled out a bottle of whisky, smashed it, releasing the whisky, and brandished the broken bottle. Birch stopped in his tracks.

'Right ... you want me ... you're going to get this. Come on then.' Eddie was breathing hard, meaning every word.

Birch knew that Eddie was quite capable of using the bottle in his face. He stood aside. 'Right then. On you go. I'm nae interferin'. Please yersel'.'

Eddie walked past him, tense, expecting to be grabbed, fully intending to lash out with the bottle if he had to.

Birch let him go on down the stairs to where his Mum sat in a parked mini, waiting.

'Oh, get knotted!' He flung the angry words at her and ran up the road to rejoin his mates.

It was the end of all parental control. He spent the days skiving school, stealing cars, stealing whatever he could, drinking and fighting. Always fighting.

One night there was a big fight between some school kids - the Powis boys and the Froghall lads. Although he was their age, Eddie had been trained in a much tougher school. The kids had never seen anybody fight like him before.

In the midst of the action Eddie picked up a big stone and threw it. Then he heard folk screaming that one of the boys had been hit in the head. To Eddie it was all in the game. If they couldn't cope with that kind of fighting, they shouldn't be there. It could happen to anybody - it was one of the risks. You had to take your chance.

Not surprisingly the Headmaster didn't quite see it that way later on. Eddie denied all knowledge of the fight but the police, who were also at the interview, knew better.

Something would have to be done about Eddie!

3

ROSSIE FARM

Eddie sat silent, refusing to co-operate as the Children's Panel considered his case. He let his Mum, who had also been summoned, do most of the talking. 'I'm only fourteen,' he thought confidently. 'They can't do anything to me.' But the members of the Panel thought otherwise. He was returned for one more night to the local Remand Home and the following morning social workers drove him forty miles south to Rossie Farm, Montrose.

'Looks like a school,' he thought as they turned in at the gates. 'I wonder what kinda place it is?'

He soon found out. Ordinary lessons did go on, but there was also gardening, bricklaying, cooking, dining-hall work and laundry. There was even some farm work with potatoes and carrots. After teatime came recreation - TV, darts, snooker, and pool. But none of these really interested Eddie. All he thought about was how he could get away. He had no intention of staying long in this place! But for the time being he would just lie low.

He did this until he got stabbed. It happened one night when he was lying in bed in the dormitory. A

boy whom Eddie didn't get on with came and
stabbed him hard in the ribs with a fork. Eddie didn't
make a sound. He wasn't about to tell what had
happened because he wanted to take his revenge in
person. So he made his way to the toilet, accompa-
nied by a torch-carrying night-watchman. There he
managed to contrive a makeshift dressing for his
wound from toilet paper. He'd get the guy who'd
done it, but later. For sure!

Soon afterwards Eddie found himself assigned to
the 'garden party'. He was shown how to use a petrol
lawnmower and told to cut the grass. 'Fine,' thought
Eddie. 'Here's my chance!'

For a while he tramped up and down the grass
after the lawnmower. Then, when he was sure no-
one was around, he tied the mower by its flex to a
tree, its motor still making a nice even purr, while he
slipped away through on to the railway line and
headed off in the direction of Arbroath, the next
town further south.

Later that evening it wasn't too difficult to break
into a butcher's shop and help himself to a few pies.
He found an old shed to sleep in and early next
morning he hitched a lift in a fish van back to
Aberdeen.

His freedom didn't last long and when the authorities caught up with him they hauled him back to
Rossie Farm.

Though not for long. For his next escape Eddie
collaborated with three other lads. Two broke into

the clothes store while Eddie and another boy got into the cookhouse and filled two black plastic bags with steak pies. Timing it carefully they 'did a shoot' dressed in civvy clothes, firing pies at each other as they ran along the railway line to freedom. What a lark! They slept rough that night near the beach and woke about 4 a.m. frozen stiff. So they boarded a rowing boat which was tied up nearby, broke up some of the wooden seating and made a fire to get themselves, and what remained of the pies, warm. It wasn't long before the cops gave chase and they were all caught.

It might have been quite a lark when you were out, but it certainly wasn't much fun when you got back! Eddie found out the hard way that there were two little cells in Rossie Farm which the Headmaster used to administer a punishment known as jump-ups - sharp strokes of a belt laid across bare buttocks! You might be awarded four or five, but sometimes as many as a dozen!

While these jump-ups never deterred Eddie from trying to escape again, they did have an inward effect. They built up the anger inside him, and the resentment against the constant restraints. This often caused him to react violently and sometimes, when he was due for punishment, they would send three men to administer it, two to hold him and one to do the belting.

One day Eddie decided he just wasn't going to accept it. He jerked himself away and did a runner, up some stairs and onto a corridor. But it was a dead end and all the windows were locked. That time he got twelve jump-ups and a week locked into a tiny cell. Yet within half an hour of his release he had broken out again, and this time he stayed out for several months.

He had a high old time - breaking and entering to steal money, clothes, drink, anything he fancied. He slept rough most of the time, but he kept himself smart by using the public toilets for a wash and shave before going into a department store to 'look at' suits. He soon learnt how to walk out wearing one of the store's new suits beneath his own coat!

He knew the police were on the look out for him though he never bothered to hide his prints when he broke in anywhere. He knew it was only a matter of time before they caught up with him, but until then he intended to enjoy himself.

He moved about between Montrose, Arbroath and Aberdeen and then decided to hitch a lift to Banff where his mother and Granda were now living quite close to each other. He travelled at night to avoid being seen and headed for Granda's house. He had no intention of going in but he knew that there was an old shed-cum-garage behind Granda's house with an old Austin Seven car inside. It would be a good place to sleep.

For a day or two he managed to feed himself by stealing food from the neighbouring houses when the folk were out. But then his Mum spotted him. In a way that made things easier, for she started to take food to him, but secretly so that neither her husband nor Granda would suspect that he was there.

But, inevitably, Granda caught sight of her crossing the yard one day with a plate of chips half-hidden under her coat.

'Eddie's in the shed,' he challenged when she came back.

'No, he's nae,' she denied. But Granda knew better.

'You'd better get him in the hoose. He's nae stayin' ootside,' the old man insisted. So Eddie moved up into the loft and stayed with them for some time. He kept out of sight as much as possible, though a few trusted visitors knew he was there.

Then one night they had a lot of visitors and somebody went to the police and told them where Eddie was.

It wasn't long before the police cars arrived. Eddie scrambled up into the loft. Lying there in the darkness he could hear the police dogs barking outside. There must be more than one, he realised. Then with a thump and a scrape the trapdoor of the loft opened and a beam of torchlight swept around the small space. Eddie froze, daring to hope that he might not be seen. And then the bobby spoke.

'Come on ... doon ye come, Murison.'

Eddie scrambled to his feet and moved towards the opening where the policeman's head was protruding. Angry at being discovered, he aimed a kick at the bobby's head, but his left leg slipped and the other foot went right through the ceiling!

Eddie was still struggling as he reached ground level. Then Granda spoke up sharply.

'Come on, that's enough! Take it as a man. Ye got yersel' into this!'

The police hustled the still struggling Eddie outside where two police dogs and more policemen were waiting. But maybe Granda was right. Maybe he should go quietly.

He spent the night in the police station and next morning a car came to drive him back to Rossie Farm. As they were passing through Aberdeen the car stopped at a red light. Quick as a flash Eddie nipped out, jumped over a fence and into the grounds of a hospital. He was away again, but not for long.

This time the police took him to the Beacon Community Centre at Bucksburn, Aberdeen. They phoned his Mum.

'I'm nae interested,' she said shortly. 'He's got his own life; he's just pleased hisself.'

What were they to do with him? Although he was only fourteen he would just have to go into Aberdeen's adult prison, Craiginches, where they could be sure of holding him until various reports could be obtained from social and psychiatric workers.

The reality of prison didn't hit Eddie until he was sitting in the Dub Box. This was a very small cell with just enough room to sit. He'd been ordered to take off his clothes and put on prison garments and left to get on with it.

All kinds of thoughts whirled round in his mind as he sat there alone. He'd hated the sound of the doors banging behind him as they entered the prison. The clicking of locks had reminded him that this wasn't just an Approved School. This was jail ... a place for hardened criminals ... and he was just a kid. There might be poofters. Who knew what they might do to him? What was he doing here? This was the end of the road! A cold fear crept over him.

But after a while his natural buoyancy helped him kick back. 'To pot with it!' he told himself. 'I'm here. I must be as bad as they are. I'll show 'em!'

The door opened to admit a man with big scars on his face. 'You all right, wee man?' he asked.

Eddie reacted in instant fury. 'Who're you calling wee man? I'm nae little! Get shot! I'm no' a mug.'

The man shrugged. 'Follow me,' he ordered. 'They've put you in B Hall.' Eddie followed the man through a door and suddenly found himself in a huge hall with long corridors of doors. Everything was strangely quiet. The men were all walking about like zombies. Many of them had slash scars on their faces, 'Mars bars' he would later learn to call them - and they were all pale from being inside so long. Eddie shivered. It felt so alien ... terrifying .... He was taken to a cell and the door locked behind him. This was it! He was in jail; a real jail - quite different from Approved School. There the cells were more like small rooms. This was all brickwork with a light stuck in the wall, a wee board for posters and a

concrete floor. He didn't need to examine the bed to
know it was filthy. The stink of urine on the dirty
blankets was unmistakable - and powerful. The new
routine started at 6 a.m. next day. Someone opened
his door, looked in, checked whether there were one
or two inmates, then banged the door shut again. He
went the whole length of the corridor ... bang, bang,
bang!

Thoroughly awakened by the racket, Eddie heard
the prison officers shouting, '35 on second, 44 on the
top, 30 on the bottom'. If the total numbers proved
nobody was missing the next cry was: 'Open 'em
up.'

Once the doors were opened Eddie found you had
to take your 'pot' along the corridor, slop it out and
wash it. Then you got water in a basin and took it
back into your cell to wash yourself. When that had
been emptied, you sat in your cell until 7.00 a.m.
when it was breakfast time. Immediately after breakfast you were locked up until 11 a.m. when you were
taken into a small yard for exercise. Locked up again
until lunch and dinner time, and after that locked up
again for the night. You were locked up for almost
23 hours a day!

For once in his life Eddie had little to do but think
- and plenty of time to do it in! Strangely enough he
didn't mind too much. He decided that, in spite of the
poor quality of food, and never having enough of it,
he would do all he could to keep himself fit. So he
gradually built up his 'score' of press-ups and in

between these he indulged in wildly aggressive fantasies. Nor did he limit his aggression to fantasy. One morning at breakfast he was given porridge, a piece of toast and jam. (Eddie's idea of a good breakfast was bacon, egg and black pudding.)

'What's that?' he growled.

'Yer breakfast. If you don't want it, don't take it.'

Don't want it? Eddie grabbed a pot of porridge and rammed it down on the unfortunate server's head. The rest of the men dived for cover. If Eddie was going on the rampage, it was best to make yourself scarce!

Eddie ran over to the tea urn and threw it down. Hot tea flooded the floor! Two Prison Officers came flying to grab him, stepped on the spilt porridge and tea and fell down. Eddie carried on throwing things as fast as he could, and for a few glorious moments there was complete chaos as the officers tried to catch the elusive offender.

Eddie thought it made a wonderful scene to look back on once they had locked him up in 'solitary' as punishment!

He soon decided that solitary was brilliant! In many ways a loner, he enjoyed the peace of a private cell. He could switch off and forget the hassle of all the other guys being around. And as he had no intention of working for them anyway, at least here he was free to lie back and daydream all day. In a funny way he could be free. His mind could be thinking of Granda ... anyone ... great plans for doing bigger jobs when he got out again ... who he might get to work with him.

It satisfied something deep inside Eddie to use his time in solitary positively. Hadn't Granda trained him always to benefit from whatever situation he was in? He certainly wasn't going to let this beat him. He was determined to get something worthwhile out of it.

It was to be the same all through his prison life. Whatever they did to him, wherever they put him, he tried to turn that situation to his own advantage. He had to do what they said - but why not benefit at the same time?

In any case, as soon as his reports came through, he'd be moving on.

4

BORSTALS AND BREAKAWAYS

The next stop was Borstal, at Polmont. And instantly, Eddie knew it was different from any place he'd been before. Very different. There was no high wall round it like Craiginches, but it was a huge building and all the windows were barred. The cells here were polished and everything else was the same - all spick and span and clean. The prison officers didn't wear uniforms but suits.

Eddie wondered what other differences he would find. What really hit him was the strict regime. Their curt way of giving orders roused instant rebellion in Eddie. 'Get your hair cut!'

'You're nae gonna cut my hair!' Eddie protested.

But they banged him down and cut his hair really short.

'Now get a shave!'

'I dinna shave.' But he had to, even though his beard had barely started to grow.

Eddie soon found that regimentation applied throughout the establishment. Whenever you were being taken anywhere, it was left! right! left! right! Like the army, Eddie thought. 'I'm nae gonna do it,' he said to himself, as he deliberately ambled along. He earned a lot of hidings that way!

There was even a drill for being moved out of your cell. The officers would open the doors and shout: 'Under your lights!' At this command the men were to stand directly under the light in their cell. 'Outside!' At this order, they went out of the door and turned to face it. There could be a hundred men standing to lock their doors. Eddie would take his time. Everything inside him rebelled at the way orders were given so he went at his own speed in spite of the shouts and threats and often knocks.

Silence was another rule. If you spoke to the guy next to you, you got put on report. Even time at the toilet was strictly limited. Eddie was often told to 'Snib it!', though he usually carried on. And he'd be on report again.

It all added up to an atmosphere of intense pressure. And it affected staff and inmates alike. Compared to Rossie Farm it was a heavy place to be. Very heavy. And the explosion was not long in coming.

It happened when all the men were in the canteen eating dinner. The officer in charge shouted: 'Murison!'

Eddie rose from the table and ran to the officer. 'Yes, sir!' The officer handed Eddie a letter and he returned to his seat.

Seconds later the cry rang out again: 'Murison!'

Eddie left the table again and ran up. 'Yes, sir!' He was handed a second letter and sent back to his seat. He threw the letter down beside the first one. They could wait until he had eaten - he was hungry! He took up his soup spoon and the steaming liquid was halfway to his mouth when the cry rang out yet again: 'Murison!'

This time Eddie just ignored him. He concentrated on eating his soup. The shout came again, but louder this time. 'MURISON!'

Eddie carried on eating, but warily, watching from the corner of his eye to see what was going to happen.

'MURISON!'

Eddie could feel all the guys round about almost holding their breath, and looking round uneasily. But he went on calmly eating his soup. He heard the prison officer walking towards him ... but still Eddie didn't stop eating. The man bent over Eddie, put his mouth close to his ear and yelled: 'M U R I S O N!'

Eddie turned towards him and said, with deliberate cheek: 'Yeh?'

'Didn't you hear me shouting your name?'

'No,' said Eddie, feigning innocence. He looked around. 'Did anybody else hear it?'

Everybody sat dumb, wondering what was going to happen. The prison officer was getting really 'hyper' and they were all apprehensive, waiting for Eddie to get pulled over the barrel.

'There's a letter,' the officer snapped. Eddie snapped too. He flung his soup bowl crashing down on the floor and stood up. 'Why did you get me down

three times for a letter when you could have just
called me down once? What's the problem with you,
pal?'

Eddie was itching to go for the guy. He kept
pushing him and pushing him some more. But the
officer wouldn't hit him. Even when Eddie invited
him to. 'Come on - hit me! HIT ME!'

But the officer resisted the temptation. So Eddie
carried on, increasingly confident, enjoying this
challenge with authority.

'What's the problem? Too many witnesses, pal?
Is that what the problem with you is? You want to go
in a cell and do something?'

This time he'd gone too far and later he regretted
it, because they *did* get him in a cell and give him a
working over. And then they locked him up for a few
more days.

In Borstal tension seemed to be in the air they
breathed and fights among the men often broke out.
Eddie and another guy were fighting one day, but
they stopped when they saw an officer approaching.
They agreed to carry on later.

Given the opportunity, Eddie decided to make
preparations. Together with another lad he broke
into a storeroom where, amongst other things, razor
blades were kept. He took a long piece of shaving
soap, broke it in half, stuck in a couple of razor
blades and slipped the lot into his pocket. Back in the
dormitory he fixed the soap and a blade to act as a
knife, capable of slashing. He hid this inside his

shirt. Then he stuffed two books behind his kidneys for protection and a couple more in front in case the other guy tried to plunge him in a vital spot. Then he strode off to keep his rendezvous with his opponent.

They had decided to fight in the toilet block where they would be more or less out of sight. They had just started going for each other, and were getting really stuck in, their heavy blows making blood flow freely, when a prison officer appeared. Immediately both men ran - Eddie back to the dormitory. He tore off his bloodstained shirt, grabbed someone else's and by the time the prison officer arrived he was sitting on his bed.

'On your feet!' Everybody in the dormitory sprang to attention beside their beds, Eddie included. The officer paced the room, and reaching Eddie, hit him an almighty swipe on his face. Eddie fell back across his bed. Anger coursed through his body, but his mind flashed a warning. 'Keep it ... keep it. This is no' the time. They're just wanting you in the cells to interrogate you. Keep quiet.'

The officer stood over Eddie. 'You tried to kill a man,' he accused.

'I never touched anybody. I dinna ken what you're talking about. I've just been sittin' here all night,' he lied.

'You slashed a guy ... you just missed him. You got him in the throat.'

'I dinna ken nothing aboot it,' Eddie insisted.

The officer walked away, leaving Eddie pretty

scared. Had he really hurt the guy as bad as the
officer said? He hadn't meant to, but he couldn't be
sure. 'What am I going to do with this one?' he
wondered. 'I could get five years for this. How am
I going to get out of it?'

The idea which came to him almost scared Eddie,
but he decided to give it a try. He went to the toilet
and retrieved a blade which he had previously hidden there. Back in the dormitory he spoke to the
other eleven lads. 'I'm gonna cut my wrist. As soon
as I cut it, you hit that bell. Get the screws in. You've
got to do this for me 'cos if they can fix this on me
I'm gonna face four or five years.'

He glanced round the group, willing them to
agree.

'OK, Eddie.'

Eddie sat down on his bed, the blade in his hand.
So far so good. But he suddenly felt apprehensive.
He hadn't a clue how to do it. What if he cut an artery
or something? What if they didn't stop the bleeding
in time?

He felt the cold sweat break out all over him as he
sat there, motionless. 'What am I gonna do? I've
told these guys I'm gonna do it. If I don't they'll
think I'm a softie.'

The mental battle lasted for several minutes but in
the end he thought: 'To pot with it! I'll go for it!'

He did. He sliced his wrist. Blood flowed. The
guys hit the bell. The door opened and officers
rushed in, grabbed Eddie and took him straight down

to the doctor. Once he was stitched up he was taken to 'solitary'. A single tiny light shone in the darkness of the cell and Eddie was ordered to sit on the one hard chair until told to move to his bed for the night.

Next morning he was up before the Governor. 'What happened?'

'I was feeling rotten and depressed. I was wanting to do away wi' myself.'

'You're a liar, Murison. I know what you did. I know that *you* know that I know that you tried to nick that guy's face.'

'But I couldn't have ...'.

'I also know that you know that I know that you broke in and got razor blades.'

'I don't know about that. But the razor blade's right 'cos I cut myself with it.'

The Governor was silent long enough for Eddie to hope his plan would work out. After all it was one man's word against another. And Eddie had eleven witnesses to prove he had cut himself. It had been a crazy stunt ... but he got away with it that time!

Days, weeks, months of the grim routine went by, but Eddie never got used to the atmosphere of fear and tension. It was especially scary at nights. Sometimes a man would cut his wrists or try to hang himself and his screams would resound through the hall. Men screamed for all sorts of reasons and their violent cries tormented Eddie as he lay on his bed trying to sleep. It was all too heavy for a lad of sixteen, he felt.

Daytime was little better. Eddie once noticed a prison officer holding a bucket. As a prisoner walked past him, the officer dropped the bucket right behind the man. PLANG! The clatter of metal on concrete shattered the air and the prisoner jumped violently. He turned, as if to punch the daylights out of the officer. 'Oh yes! Go for him!' the watching prisoners screamed inwardly, silently. The man turned away and nothing happened.

But the incident proved to Eddie that the officers were also affected by the tension. Officers and men alike were paranoid.

Some time before his release Eddie was given Training For Freedom. Dressed in Borstal uniform he travelled daily by bus to the local hospital to help with the patients.

Eddie found that some of the old men were real characters and he enjoyed doing what he could for them. Some of them were heavy smokers, and were often short of money to buy cigarettes. So Eddie would 'oblige' by accepting their transistor, or anything else they might want to dispose of, paying them for it and then sending the article home for resale, and hopefully profit.

One day he was on his way back to the Borstal and he had a fiver in his pocket. So he and a pal went into a pub for a quick pint. This was great! Eddie was just about to raise the second pint to his lips when he noticed a prison officer sitting in a corner. He immediately ducked his head.

'We'd better go. There's a screw watching us and I don't want to lose my remission. If we get caught we'll get the full whack.'

They slipped out and ran for the bus back to Borstal, just in time for dinner.

But the prison officer caught up with Eddie. 'You've been drinking?' he asked.

'Yes sir! One pint.' It was no good denying it.

'Why?'

'I was depressed and I thought if I had one pint I could just take it.'

'Right. Get him into the cells,' the man barked.

A group of officers seized him and carried him, struggling, down the stairs, taking care to bump him as much as they could on the way. It was the end of Eddie's training for freedom!

But with the end of his sentence freedom came at last. And Eddie knew what he had to do. For he had received news from his mother. Bad news. Granda was ill. Very ill. He had to go and see him before it was too late.

5

MARRIAGE

'Yer Granda's nae weel. An' he's hopin' tae see ye soon.'

Eddie stuffed his mother's letter back into his pocket as the train carried him north to Aberdeen and then on to Banff and Granda.

It was a shock to see the old man looking so frail. He had always been so strong, so full of life. But Granda was pleased to see Eddie. Pleased, but realistic.

'I've only lasted this long 'cos I wanted to see ye again,' he murmured when the stocky teenager stood beside his bed.

A few days later Granda died. Nobody was surprised. But his death hit Eddie like a body blow. He stumbled blindly outside into the yard and across to the shed. Recent rain had made the place into a morass of mud. Eddie flung himself headlong into it. What did it matter that he was wearing a completely new outfit provided by his uncle? Suit, shirt, tie, sweater - all became filthy with mud as Eddie rolled around, as deep, angry sobs were wrenched from his body.

As he kicked and groaned and punched the ground all kinds of thoughts whirled in his head. He remembered the rabbit he'd lost long ago, and the toys. And it all seemed to be mixed up with losing Granda. Why? Why was he always a loser?

His Uncle Don came outside after a while to see if he could help.

'I wish I'd went wi' him,' Eddie raged, still sobbing. 'I wish I could die. Then I'd be wi' him right now.'

'Och away and grow up!' Don said brusquely. He had no words to comfort Eddie, so he left him alone again with his rage and his grief.

The night before Granda was buried the family all stayed up for the customary wake. The room they were sitting in was in semi-darkness and some of the men were asking Eddie about his time in Borstal.

One of Eddie's almost unconscious habits was to run a comb through his hair, so at one point he rose and walked over to the mirror, comb in hand. As he looked into the glass he froze. For one split second, he saw Granda's face looking back at him! He sat down quickly, very shaken. When at last he could explain, the rest of the family accepted his story easily. They believed in the supernatural. To them it was real. It fitted in with the stories they told.

Eddie went along with their beliefs, but at the same time he was puzzled. When he had seen the face he had felt an overwhelming sensation of fear, one which had literally made the hairs on his scalp bristle. But why should he be scared at seeing Granda's face? Nothing about Granda had ever been scary. Eddie was confused.

They buried Granda the following day in Banff. Something very precious had gone out of Eddie's life forever.

The future lay blank before him. What was he going to do now? At sixteen what schooling he'd had was over so he accepted his mother's offer and agreed to stay on in Banff for a while. He might even get a job.

In that, he was fortunate. Painter and decorator Bill Anderson offered to take him on as an apprentice. 'I'll give you a chance because you've told me the truth about being in prison. I know you've had problems.'

Eddie realised he had been lucky to be taken on at all at sixteen. Apprentices usually started at fifteen. So he stuck it for a while. But he was used to having far more money at his disposal. His weekly wages seemed a mere pittance by comparison. So he gradually started supplementing them in the old way, taking what he fancied. Especially cars.

He was handy enough when it came to changing number plates and when he needed a tax disc he would fashion his own from a beer bottle label. Insurance he didn't bother with. He found he could drive around for months without anybody realising he had a nicked car. And a car was a necessity when you were 'on a job'. You had to have some way of transporting the goods you managed to remove from people's houses or wherever. And Eddie was discovering some much larger houses to raid, with ever richer pickings.

Of course, in time, he got caught. And he found himself up on several charges: theft, driving without insurance, road tax or MOT. He was awarded nine months for each offence to run concurrently and was sent to a Young Offenders prison at Friarton, Perth.

This was something like the Borstal he'd been in before except that the inmates were a bit older. There was the same regimented approach, the same hassle and fights between boys from different places, so Eddie managed to get up to quite a bit of 'mischief'.

But he found it was a great place to learn and he was not slow to make the most of the 'education' offered. In Perth he learned how to 'do' alarm systems, quietly putting them out of action. He discovered how to rip the backs off safes and how to use plastic explosives safely. 'Some of these guys are really talented and gifted at getting into places,' he confided to a newcomer. 'You can learn a lot here.'

It was in Perth that he first became aware of 'the System'. In Rossie Farm and Borstal you had been up against people. You had to watch what you were doing for fear of them. Here it was a system you were up against. You learned to react against it instead of against any one person. You learned to fight the system, even though you knew you'd never break it.

But you could try to beat it as often as possible.

The same system applied in Barlinnie where Eddie was sent for later offences. When he arrived there he found there were four floors of cells each for a different grade of sentence. The ground floor housed men who were serving 60 days. The next landing was for prisoners with a sentence of up to 6 months. The third landing was for men serving between 9 months and two to three years and the top landing was for 'Lifers'.

Eddie's sentence was 9-12 months depending on his behaviour. But somehow he found himself in a top floor cell with the lifers.

'What am I doing up here?' he wondered. 'This is a set-up to get me.'

But he soon found a couple of guys he could be pally with and they used to amuse themselves by giving the staff as much hassle as they could. One ploy was to get hold of a PP9 battery, snake along the floor of the top gallery and aim it at a Prison Officer down below. It didn't matter whether you hit him or not. It just added to the hassle. It was one way of getting back at the system and no-one down below could ever see who was throwing things, so you were safe enough.

It was a harder jail than the others Eddie had been in. Probably the toughest of the lot, he decided. But he couldn't let the other guys think he was a mug ... so he put on a swagger, deliberately assuming a toughness he didn't feel, determined to let anybody

and everybody know that he was no wimp! When he
had still six months left to serve he was moved from
Barlinnie to Edinburgh Young Offenders. Here there
were two halls each with different coloured shirts,
red and blue. Good conduct enabled you to progress
from one colour to the other, though Eddie never did!

Perhaps he was too incident prone! Like the time
when one guy kept giving him funny looks whenever they passed each other.

'What's going on here?' Eddie wondered. Whatever it was would need to be sorted out - and quick.
So Eddie challenged the guy to meet him in his cell
at 4.30 p.m. that day after work. As soon as the door
banged shut behind them the two youths tore into
each other - fists, the 'heid', the boot - the lot. Their
hair was standing on end, their shirts ripped and
there was blood everywhere. Then the door opened
and a prison officer stood there.

'How's it going?' Eddie asked in as normal a tone
as he could muster.

'What are you two doing?' the officer demanded.

'Oh, nothing. I fell over, but I'm all right Sir.' (In
this jail you had to address the officers as 'Sir'.)

'You two were fighting.' It was a statement.

'We wasna', Sir.'

'Well how come you're in such a mess?'

'I fell doon the stair and my nose was bleeding
....'

The officer cut short Eddie's speech. 'Well I
think you *were* fighting. You're on report.'

'On report for what? I never done nothing to get caught for ....'

His protest was no use. Eddie was hauled off to hospital to have the damage to his knuckles repaired and he returned with his right hand swathed in bandages. This provided a fine excuse for not shaving. But the officers were not going to let him get away with that.

'Shave!' he was ordered.

'I canna. I'm right-handed and my hand's all bandaged.'

'You will shave.' The order was repeated.

'But I've hurt my hand. I canna, Sir.'

'Right. You're on report for refusing to take an order.'

'But I'm not refusing, Sir. I want to see the Medical Officer.'

In front of the Governor next day he was asked why he was not shaving.

'My hand's IN PLASTER, man. Have I to spell it out for you?'

'But you're refusing. You could still shave. If *my* hand was in plaster, *I'd* be able to shave.'

'Well, I'm nae as double-jointed as you so-and-sos,' Eddie retorted cheekily. A sharp slap stung his face. They'd got it in for him, Eddie decided. Well, he'd find some way to show them.

One way he found to express his resentment was by starting small fires. Nothing big enough to do damage, but enough to get the staff worried ...

enough to let them know who was doing it but without their being able to prove anything.

He would take a bin from the landing and fill it with anything that would make smoke ... dried stuff out of mattresses for example. Once it was lit he'd walk away and comment to the nearest officer: 'There's an awfu' smell o' smoke up here, man.'

The officers were not fooled. But without proof, they couldn't always manage to pin things on him.

Not all Eddie's activity in Edinburgh was negative. He did quite a lot of keep-fit training - press-ups and weight training. And it was equally important to keep yourself 'psyched up' mentally - when your cell door opened you never knew whether there might be a guy coming flying in with a knife or intent on some other kind of hassle. You needed eyes in the back of your head when you walked about the jail. You really needed to know what was going on.

But jail sentences always came to an end sooner or later, as one did when Eddie was nineteen. He made his way to Aberdeen and went into a pub called East Neuk. He knew this was a really tough pub. Walking up to the bar he placed his order.

'A pint of wa'er and fill it wi' salt.'

'What?' The barmaid stared at him in disbelief. Eddie repeated his order, adding: 'I've got a sair stomach. I dinna ken what it is, maybe an ulcer. I've heard that's good for it.'

It was a load of rubbish, but he liked the look of the lassie and at least now he had her interest. As they chatted on he discovered that her brother owned the pub. It wasn't long before he was going steady with Marion and was taken on to work as a 'bouncer' in the pub. The job proved harder and rougher than he'd imagined, sorting out fights or physically removing men who were dead drunk - and heavy!

But there were also bonuses - of a kind. Men who had known Eddie in the past would turn up, and Eddie now had the power to say whether or not to allow them in.

'You're nae gettin' in,' he'd say, when he felt like it.

'I'll buy you a pint, Eddie.'

'Right. You can get in.'

Obviously exchanges like this were Eddie's passport to drunkenness. Other guys would arrive who knew Eddie had a jail record. They would have 'goods' to offer on the cheap.

Once Eddie was offered a superb watch for a mere £30. He took it like a shot.

'I hinna got the money but I'll gi'e it to ye later,' he promised - but with no intention of ever paying. The guy came several times to collect his money, but each time Eddie fobbed him off with excuses.

Then one night the man returned with two or three of his pals. 'I want my money and I want it *now*!' he demanded.

Eddie knew he meant it and responded accordingly. He flew right across the floor, rammed the man with his head, got him down and starting kicking him as he lay on the floor. Then he rolled him

down the stairs, pulled him outside on to the street
and began to bounce his head off the cobblestones.
Alternately he punched his victim and crashed his
head on the granite blocks.

Marion and her brother came out and forced their
way through the small knot of onlookers.

'Stop it! Lay off him. You're going to kill him!'
they shouted.

But Eddie paid no heed. As if driven by some
powerful inward force he kept on assaulting his
victim until he was finally dragged off.

Marion was under no illusions about the kind of
man Eddie was as their courtship continued, especially as he moved into her flat before they got married.
But they were strongly attracted to each other so that,
when Eddie was facing a court case in Banff she
went with him to the hearing. On the bus she tried to
reassure him. 'I'll write to you when you're in jail,
Eddie. I'll wait for you. However long it is.'

But Eddie refused to be reassured. 'This is rubbish,' he thought. 'I know what'll happen once I'm
in there. She'll send me a 'Dear John', even though
she *is* expecting.'

Later they sat close together in the courtroom,
silently waiting for the hammer. The judge looked
them both up and down before pronouncing sentence. He made a few general comments on the case
and then concluded: 'This time I believe you are
genuinely sorry for what you have done. And because you intend to get married and your girlfriend

is expecting I will give you a two year sentence - deferred.'

For the first time in his life Eddie said 'Thank you' to a judge, and meant it. It was the first time anybody had been willing to give him another chance. He determined not to waste it.

He did make an honest attempt to settle down, especially when his son, Peter James, was born. He managed to find first one job and then another, but the sort of work he got never paid the kind of money Eddie felt he needed. And it was just so easy to supplement it in the way he knew best - stealing it from other people.

Not that Marion knew where all the money came from. Eddie led her to believe that he earned it during the long hours he spent away from home. He would give her money as if he were receiving a normal wage and as long as he supplied the money he expected her to ask no questions.

Eddie resented questions. He wanted to live life *his* way - go where he wanted *when* he wanted; drink when he wanted and as much as he wanted. And if a pretty girl were willing to go out with him, well why not? It was a hopeless way to conduct a marriage, but at the least suggestion that he should stay home more and stop his heavy drinking sessions, Eddie would go off in a rage. 'I canna cope wi' that,' he'd tell his pals. 'Prison's better. Once you're in your cell the door's shut and that's you. Naebody bothers you.'

After a while Eddie decided to become officially self-employed. Unknown to Marion he borrowed money from her brother and other friends, bought himself a big black van, and became a slater. But that was only part of the story. As he was working on the roof slates he'd look through the windows to see what was available. Then he would make a return visit at night and remove jewellery, videos or whatever he fancied.

When another baby was on the way they moved to another house in Stewart Park, but Eddie's behaviour didn't change. Marion became suspicious and, when he came home very late one night, she was waiting.

'Where have you been?' she demanded. And then, when Eddie refused to answer, 'You were out with somebody else.'

'No, I wasna',' Eddie lied. She couldn't prove it, so why worry? But he knew his marriage was in tatters. Marion was doing all she could, but he just couldn't cope with being married and tied down. It was too much. He moved out and went back to his mother who now lived in Grandholm Estate.

Shortly afterwards Eddie's second son, Stewart, was born. He saw the baby only twice. And then Marion made the break.

'Wi' all your carryin' on and your hassle, I canna cope. I don't want to know you.'

And that was it. The marriage was finished.

6

ANGRY YOUNG MAN

Twenty-one can be a wonderful age. Not long ago it heralded the entry to official adulthood. But for Eddie it marked his entry into an adult prison, and the 'key of the door' turned behind him in Craiginches, Aberdeen after yet another offence against society.

At first Eddie found it a scary situation - like moving into zombieland. The prison officers acted so differently - they didn't order you around, constantly giving directions as they had in Young Offenders. In fact the whole routine was different.

You got up at 6 a.m., had breakfast and went straight to work until the 12 o'clock lunch. From 1 to 2 p.m. you had exercise and then worked again until 4 o'clock teatime. At 4.30 p.m. you were locked up for the night. Only after three months were you allowed evening recreation such as TV or snooker. So Eddie found he had hours to spend sitting on a chair, thinking.

'What a waste it all is! Here I am back in prison and what have I to show for my life?' he mused despondently. 'My marriage is finished, and even though I have two sons, I might never see them again.' The feeling of hurt and loss bit deep now that he had time to think about it. Why was it that he seemed to destroy everything he put his hand on? Why did he always lose the people he loved - or just throw them away? However long he thought about it, he couldn't work out the reason. He only knew that his whole situation depressed him. But what could he do?

And then one day a tiny incident triggered an unexpectedly violent response.

It happened when a prison officer came in to his cell. Seeing a packet of biscuits on Eddie's table he helped himself to one. Eddie said nothing, but inwardly he was seething with resentment. He almost told the man where to go, but somehow managed to hold his tongue.

When the officer had gone Eddie strode across to the sheds where the men were working. 'What's wrong, Eddie?'

'I'm fed up, that's what!' Eddie spat the words out angrily. 'Look, you guys move away. Something's gonna happen.'

He quickly spotted a couple of men he knew, one serving a life sentence. He'd know how to help.

'I'm wanting to do a bit of damage. What would be the best thing to use?'

'What about that big iron bar?' the man suggested, indicating the head-height metal support used for making Army camouflage nets - one of the regular occupations in the prison.

Eddie checked it. It would suit him fine. When the time came. At two o'clock when all the men were working, Eddie walked into the long barnlike workshed. In one half men were sitting on stools, using knitting machines. In the other half men were working on the camouflage nets. Rising from shoulder height a series of thick, unbreakable glass windows separated the two working areas. Only three or four of the men knew about his plan and they were surreptitiously watching him, waiting for something to happen. Sitting on a stool, Eddie himself was waiting.

He hadn't quite figured out exactly when he was going to move but he could feel the gut reaction building up inside. His nerves always felt the same whenever he was going to do anything nasty. Part of him was dead scared, but this only helped him to psyche himself up for the moment of action. It came. He flew off his seat, gave the iron bar a hefty kick and, using all his strength, ripped it out of the wall. For a second he stood there, panting, holding the solid metal bar in the air.

Then, before anybody knew what was going on, he started smashing the windows in the glass divider screen. Splintering glass showered in all directions as he worked his way along, swinging the iron bar with such force that the wooden frames were knocked out along with the glass. Prisoners ran as they were ordered outside. Riot bells clamoured and squads of prison officers came flying in. Chaos reigned as

Eddie continued to smash his way along the heavy glass windows.

He even took time to shout to the officers: 'Come near me and *you're* gettin' it!'

Few approached, he noticed. They were intent on getting the place clear before any other prisoners joined in with him.

Then suddenly the shed seemed to be a mass of uniforms as the prison officers closed in a big circle round Eddie.

'If I drop this bar, I've had it,' Eddie realised, breathing hard from his efforts. 'They'll murder me! Oh no! What's gonna happen?'

But he stuck to his defiant stance. In the midst of the broken glass he continued to shout threats. 'Any of you come near me and I'm gonna let you have it. End of story!'

Then an officer known as Tattie Jim took a few steps towards him. Eddie swung the bar high over his head. He was all ready to lash out and crash his weapon over the man's head. But something made him pull back.

'You're nae worth it,' he muttered, flinging the bar down to the ground. In the nick of time he'd realised what the consequences would be if he killed a prison officer. It just wasn't worth it.

Minutes later he was hustled into a silent cell, strip-searched and left to reclothe himself.

'This is where it's gonna happen,' he thought fearfully, knowing that even though the cell was not padded, men could do what they liked to him and no-one would hear his cries.

Dinner came, and with it an opportunity. Eddie ate the food and decided he could use the metal tray as a weapon. 'If they're gonna do me, I'll tak' one o' them wi' me,' he determined. When the prison officer returned for the tray, Eddie had a surprise message waiting for him. It was written on the walls - in blood! Cursing and swearing, the officer retreated in search of reinforcements. What would happen now? Eddie wondered.

The knock and polite words which followed took him, in turn, by surprise.

'Eddie, it's me - Gordon.' Eddie recognised the medical officer's voice. They talked through the door for several minutes and eventually Eddie was calm enough for the men outside to open the door.

The sight of the blood-scrawled walls alarmed them, and Eddie was still bleeding! How badly they didn't know.

From inside the cell Eddie shouted threats. 'You come in here and I'm gonna have you.' But they came in anyway and after a short struggle overpowered him and bore him off to the medical room for treatment. Afterwards they stuck him in the Pink Suite.

The Pink Suite was a very narrow cell with two sets of doors at the entrance. As Eddie was thrown inside the appalling stench of human excrement hit him. He looked around. There was a narrow bed,

with no blankets, and a chamber pot. Above his head
was a pane of thick glass. 'What now?' he thought
miserably, sitting in all the muck. And when his meal
came: 'How'm I gonna eat with this stink?'

Later on he was returned to a normal cell, but his
anger at the system and the threats he felt from
inmates and prison officers alike brought on yet
another reaction.

Once the cell door was shut, he barricaded himself in.

Mentally he spoke to the authorities. 'Right -
you've got me in this room, but that's all. You're
having nothing else. I'm nae gonna work for you.
I'm nae even gonna eat for you. As far as you're
concerned, I'm nae here. My mind's ootside and I'm
goin' awa' to sleep for the rest of my sentence ...
cheerio.'

His refusal to work brought a reminder from the
Governor. 'If you don't work, you're gonna be on a
day-to-day. That means you lose your remission.
Every day you won't work you lose one day and
you'll end up doing the whole nine month sentence.
Suit yourself.'

Eddie did. His hunger strike reduced his weight
from 14 stones to 11 before he started to eat again.
And he still refused to work.

The mind-games, the hassles, the tensions, the
fights continued for the rest of his sentence. Sometimes, at the height of his violence, Eddie realised
that he was totally confused. It was as if he was

somehow inwardly forced to do things that he wouldn't normally do. He would think: 'I dinna want to do that, but I've *got* to do that.' What was driving him? Eddie just didn't know.

Released once more Eddie went to stay with his Mum in Aberdeen. At that time her husband was working as gardener on Crombie's Grandholm Estate and she was working in the house. It was a contact which would soon prove useful to Eddie, for he had set his heart on getting a motor bike.

He went round the showrooms and selected the model he wanted - a Suzuki 125. All he needed now was money. He approached his mother.

'Would you ring the big hoose, Mum, and ask the lady if she'll see me?'

An appointment was fixed and Eddie duly arrived.

'Can I have a word with you, Julia?' he asked, bold as brass.

'Come on in,' she replied. 'What is it you want?'

'I'm thinking of buying a motorbike,' Eddie explained, and then went on to tell her about his lack of money. 'I was wondering if you would act as my guarantor?'

Julia smiled. 'I know you've been in and out of trouble so many times, Eddie,' she said. 'I'd like to help you. I'll be your guarantor.' She approached the garage only to find that they refused to accept her as guarantor, saying that because of certain regulations they would need her husband to take the responsibil-

ity. This angered Julia so much that she sent for
Eddie again and together they went to the garage
where she bought him not just the motorbike, but
crash helmet, gloves and jacket to go with it. She
even paid his first insurance!

It was not to be a gift - Eddie agreed to repay her
in fortnightly instalments. And he really intended to,
because he felt so good about the whole thing. But
he only managed the first few instalments, and the
repayments fell by the way when he stole a CB and
became infatuated with the new hobby.

He and his brother Bill stayed up till all hours
either speaking or listening, enjoying their contact
with complete strangers. One night when Bill was
operating the CB a woman's voice answered him.
Eddie grabbed the mike.

'Hey, you've got a real sexy voice. What about an
eyeball?'

'Now?' the voice queried. 'It's two o'clock in the
morning!'

'So what?' said Eddie. 'Tell me where I can pick
you up and I'll come flying on the bike.'

Minutes later Eddie roared off to meet the owner
of the sexy voice at the roundabout near Dyce
airport. It did occur to him on the way that she might
not show up - it was a bit of a crazy stunt. But she was
there all right and she was not alone - her friend and
an aunt were with her. What's more she looked as
good as she'd sounded, Eddie decided.

Sally was up from England for a week's holiday,

staying with her friend's aunt. Eddie made sure he saw plenty of her during that week and he even went back to London with her for a further week. Their acquaintance deepened so swiftly that he was able to persuade her to return to Aberdeen and live with him at his Auntie Tricia's house.

It wasn't long before Sally became pregnant, so they got married, and went to live in a Corporation flat. Then Eddie fell into the old routine of heavy drinking and going out with other women, though he kept as much as he could from Sally.

A baby daughter, Anna, was born in July. Unknowingly she was to be the cause of another incident in Eddie's career of violence.

One of the neighbours had a habit of closing his door very loudly whenever he came home. This would wake Eddie's baby and she would start screaming. This annoyed Eddie.

'If he bangs that door again, I'll *have* him,' he determined.

Sure enough next day the man came home and banged his door shut. Eddie didn't wait to hear the baby's cries, but went flying to the door with a knife. He collared the guy and started punching him in the head.

Almost immediately two policemen appeared at the door. The drink inside Eddie infused him with boldness and for some reason he took exception to their headgear. 'Either take your hats off or I'll knock 'em off!' he threatened.

The next thing he knew he was in his neighbour's house and the police were trying to get him quietened down.

'The guy's not wanting to press charges,' the police said. 'He's scared. But we'll take you to the hospital and get your hand seen to, and that's it.'

Eddie didn't believe them. Once they got him outside they'd take him to the Station and charge him he felt sure. But they managed to convince him in the end and he allowed them to take him off to hospital to get his hand dressed. How it had got into such a mess he couldn't imagine.

Next day Sally put him in the picture.

'You had a good drink in you,' she said, 'and when the guy banged the door you set off after him. But you didn't really get out - I stopped you. You had a knife in your hand and the way your face was twisted I could see you were gonna kill the guy. I stood in front of the door - you actually put the knife at my throat and said that you'd stab me to get out.'

She paused, remembering the horror of the situation. Then she went on with the story. 'I stood there because I didn't have much choice. Either you were gonna do something daft and get 'lifed up' or else get me. So I took a chance. I stood you out. You dropped the knife, but you got outside the door and began to use your fists. Once or twice you missed the guy and hit the wall. That's how your knuckles got in that state.'

But if Sally was loyal to him, Eddie did not return

the compliment. He drank heavily, went out with other women when it suited him, and acquired most of his money by stealing. He did get caught and charged for some of his thefts, but usually managed to get bail. Not that he let a little thing like bail curb his activities.

And somehow he managed to keep it all from Sally. One night he took her and another couple out for a slap-up meal on the proceeds. The other man was, like himself, out on bail. On the way back to the house the man warned him to expect the police. 'Somebody's grassed us off,' he said.

Once they got home Eddie loaded his stolen car with the stolen goods and went off and sold them to another of his friends. Then he took the number plates off the car, dumped them and set fire to the vehicle.

The police came to investigate and chased Eddie through Seton Park where he managed to slip them in spite of the full moon. Maybe it was that very moon which inspired Eddie to do something really unusual for him.

'If there is a God,' he said, looking up at the shining disc, 'I want to stay with my family - just one more night.' It wasn't much of a prayer, but God answered it. Eddie slept peacefully until six o'clock the following morning when loud knocks announced the arrival of the police. 'Who is it?'

'The milkman.' Eddie's Mum was staying with them and she opened the door. It was the CID. They ran through to where Eddie was lying in bed and jumped on top of him.

'Wait a minute,' he protested, trying to get up.

'OK. Get dressed. We've a warrant to search your house.'

So they did, but found nothing. Eddie had taken care of that. He was charged with theft, but released on bail again.

Meanwhile Eddie had been doing his own investigations and had managed to discover who had grassed on him. His next step was to find the man, and he was determined to do it.

One day, in the Powis shopping centre, Eddie met the culprit face to face. Within seconds he had flicked out a knife and held it at the terrified man's throat. Minutes passed as the two men stood there, looking into each other's eyes. Eddie was unconscious of the crowds passing by. He was overwhelmed by a sudden feeling of power. How good it felt to have such *power* ... the authority to take a man's life.

The man shivered but dared not move, the knife point pricking his throat.

'You're nothing,' Eddie said finally, disgust in his voice, as he continued to hold the knife steady. 'You're all wind - you're a grass. I'm gonna plunge you.'

But somehow he didn't. After several minutes he gave the guy a slap in the face. 'On your bike,' he ordered. 'You're no worth it, mate. Away ye go.'

As the man scuttled away, Eddie felt sickened inside ... sickened about what he was like. Somehow he didn't feel good any more. He was always getting deeper into trouble than he wanted and right now it made him want to puke.

Not that he would let anybody know how he felt, especially his mates across the road who had been watching the whole episode, waiting for the guy to go down. To them he pretended everything was great.

The incident earned Eddie a charge of threatening and intimidating a witness. He denied all knowledge and though he was questioned repeatedly there was no proof. It was just one man's word against another's. The passers-by chose not to talk.

But Eddie was sentenced to two and a half years in Saughton prison, and this time he started by behaving well, hoping to get out quicker and perhaps even get parole. Later he was transferred to Dumfries where he managed to wangle a job in the bakery. He enjoyed the work and even managed to make a bit of money.

It was in Dumfries that Sally visited him.

With Eddie in prison, she had had time to think. She was disillusioned with him, hating his lying and drinking. So she decided to go back to live in England to be near her parents. She let their house go and moved south with her baby. Once settled, she came to Dumfries to visit Eddie.

At the time Eddie was on Valium to help control

his fighting tendencies. The drug slurred his speech,
and Sally could make no sense of what he said to her.
It wasn't long before he started receiving letters
which aroused his suspicions.

'Something's no' right,' he muttered, as he read.
But the letters continued to arrive, though at growing
intervals, and he consoled himself as each one was
read to him that at least it wasn't that most dreaded
of all letters, a Dear John. Not yet.

In the end the letters stopped arriving. Then, on
Christmas Day, he was handed a letter in his cell. It
was from Sally. The gist of it was in the final
paragraph.

'The last time I saw you, you were stoned out of
your mind. It's obvious you don't want to change, so
we'll just call it quits.'

The dreaded Dear John had come at last!

7

FROM DARKNESS TO LIGHT

Rejection, regret and sheer rage hit Eddie as he stared at the sheet of paper in his hand. He'd half expected it for ages, but why should it come *now* when things were going so much better for him in jail? He was even enjoying his kitchen work and managing to get good reports - apart from the once or twice he'd hit a guy. He'd really tried to calm down hoping he might get out on parole. So why this?

'And how can I get out on parole if she's no' wantin' me?' he asked himself desperately. 'And what about my daughter? If she's taken her to England, will I ever see her again?'

Black misery settled over Eddie. And then he remembered it was Christmas Day. 'But you don't get letters in prison on Christmas Day,' he thought. 'Then how come ...?'

Eddie grabbed the letter again and looked at the date. It had been posted several days earlier. Even allowing for the Christmas rush, it must have been lying around in the prison, Eddie decided. He slammed his fist on the table.

'They've done it on purpose,' he raged. 'They kept this 'Dear John' until today on purpose. They wanted to hurt me. They're just *animals*!'

The more he thought about it the more he managed to convince himself that everybody was out to hurt him. Despair drove his hurt-crazed mind beyond rational thought as he paced his cell like a caged animal, psyching himself up for action. He hit the bell. Somebody would answer for this! When the door opened, several prison officers were standing outside, ready for action.

'What is it? What is it?' they enquired.

Eddie let rip, shouting and swearing, spewing out his hurt and anger for all to hear. Men in neighbouring cells heard the uproar and began to bang on their doors.

'What is it about, Eddie?'

'Screw the heid, Eddie?'

'I'm away for a cuppa tea,' Eddie said suddenly, and stormed off down the stairs.

Anger still boiled inside him and all sorts of mad schemes flashed through his mind as he went to the kitchen. Should he cook up a solution of boiling water laced heavily with sugar and throw it in the officers' faces? No. He'd do something worse than that ... something which would be worth being punished for!

He decided on a different plan. He went back up to his cell and just shut up. Instead of arguing and swearing, he stayed dead quiet. When anyone came and asked him if he was all right, he didn't reply. Different people came and spoke pleasantly to him, willing to listen and try to help, but they all got the same response. Silence.

The Governor prescribed three days in the punishment cells, after which he was judged fit to return to work in the kitchen. But his mind continued to focus on what harm he could do. There was one prison officer he hated particularly - a man who had a weakness for drink and kept a store of it hidden away. Maybe he would be the one to go for? What had he to lose? He'd get a long jail sentence, but what had he to go out for? He didn't have a single person out there now who could make life worth living ... no-one who cared.

The officer he had his eye on worked with him in the kitchen as a cook, so Eddie started to keep a watch on his movements. The man soon sensed his hostility and became very nervy. Eddie's pals also knew what was going on in his mind and when they saw him standing with one of the long, steel kitchen knives in his hand, they would persuade him to hand it over.

'Away up the stairs, Eddie,' they'd advise. It was behaviour like this which sometimes resulted in Eddie being put back in a cell for a night to quieten him down. Unfortunately it did not always have this effect!

These special cells had cardboard tables and chairs and once, when Eddie was locked in there, he suddenly felt as if his whole being was about to explode. He jumped up, took the table and kicked it, ripped it and started stotting his head off the wall.

A prison officer quickly came to see what was happening.

'Get it oot ... get it oot o' your system,' he urged. Eddie continued to dive about on the floor, finding a strange sort of release in saying all kinds of stupid things. And then he clammed up again. He was returned to his cell.

Tension never left him in those days. The smallest thing could cause him to flare up. One day an inmate passed by and spoke with an English accent. That was enough for Eddie. Wasn't his wife English? - and look what she'd done to him! Without warning he jumped out and grabbed the guy, threw him into a cell and started kicking him and punching him in the face. This time he ended in a cell with three prison officers.

'Take off your clothes.' The words were spoken in a calm enough tone.

Eddie said nothing. But he made no move to undress.

'Take off your clothes.' Eddie ignored the order.

He was still standing motionless when the officers pounced on him and the cell became a wrestling heap of men. Eddie bit and kicked - in fact each side got a few cracks in - and they still didn't manage to get his clothes off.

Then, without warning, the officers went out,

leaving Eddie sitting there on the floor. For the whole of the rest of the day he just sat there, bang, bang, banging the door to let them know he was still resisting.

Next day Eddie was on report. Escorted by prison officers, he was taken to a small room to be interviewed by the prison Governor and his deputy. He was charged with assaulting an inmate and causing problems with the staff.

'Have you anything to say?'

'Nothing to say.' It was his favourite response.

As a result he spent most of the next forty days in solitary confinement. This suited Eddie. Maybe he could sort out his thoughts now. But all he could think of was his wrecked marriage, his failure to get parole, and the fact that he still had another twelve months to go. It was a black prospect. One thing was sure, he would make things as hard as he could for the prison staff for the rest of his time! He could not have guessed how an unexpected visitor would revolutionise his plans.

Eddie was in his cell and had just started eating his evening meal of mince, tatties, and bread, with a big mug of tea to follow, when a visitor arrived. It was a Church of Scotland minister, the Rev Bill McKenzie. He came in, greeted Eddie and said he had come to talk about Jesus.

'But I want to ha'e my grub,' Eddie thought, eyeing the stranger.

But he said nothing. There was something about

the guy that made him feel he might be worth listening to.

'You want to eat your dinner?' McKenzie asked.

'It's all right.' Eddie suddenly found his dinner could wait after all. He was more hungry for conversation than for food, and there was something about this guy which appealed to Eddie.

So the meal slowly went cold as the two men sat and talked together.

'Jesus really wants to come into your life ...' McKenzie began.

'But look at me!' Eddie interrupted. Might as well let him have it straight. 'My life's in a mess, pal. I've naethin'.'

'I want to be honest with you, Eddie. Jesus came into the world around Christmas time and it wasn't easy for him either. He had a lot of suffering in his life. He didna' hae a roof over his heid ....'

As he listened to what McKenzie said about Jesus, Eddie found he couldn't feel sorry for himself any more. But he didn't want the guy to go on speaking about Jesus. He wanted to speak about *himself*!

'God told me to come and see you because he loves you and wants to help you, Eddie,' McKenzie went on.

Suddenly Eddie found he was pouring out the sorry story of his life and wrecked marriage. McKenzie listened to it all and then offered to write to Sally to see if things could be sorted out.

But Eddie was adamant. 'Just leave it,' he said. 'It

would be a waste of time. She's made her decision. Just leave it.'

'O.K. If that's what you want,' McKenzie said, rising to his feet. 'But I'll be back.' Before he left he handed Eddie a booklet. 'I'll leave this with you to read,' he said as the officer came to open the door.

Eddie looked at the booklet, *Journey Into Life*.

'If God really was alive like you said,' he thought, 'he'd have told you I dinna ken how to read, pal. What a joke!'

For several minutes he sat staring at the cream painted brick walls, conscious of a strangely different atmosphere in the cell. Had it anything to do with McKenzie? Or this book?

Unsettled he threw the book into the corner. It was a heap of rubbish and he couldn't read it anyway. Still conscious of the altered atmosphere he started doing press-ups. Maybe it would relieve the sense of anger building up inside him. Anger and fear. That guy had somehow shown him love, a love that Eddie feared because he couldn't understand it. How could one guy love another? There was something really queer here.

Eddie began to feel annoyed that he had shared more with him than he had ever done with anyone in his life before. Why had he done it? A renewed sense of anger incited him to put everything he'd got into the press-ups. He was really psyching himself up now. He started running on the spot, expending all his energy.

Then he rang the bell and asked to go to the toilet. Four prison officers escorted him as usual. On the way back Eddie spotted a heap of books lying on a table so he grabbed one, slipped it inside his shirt and went back to the cell.

Once inside he spelt out the title: *Hooked*. At that stage his reading was at the 'c-a-t, d-o-g' stage - longer words were a mystery to him. But somehow he picked up that book and read it from cover to cover! It took all night, but he read without stopping and managed to finish the whole book. It was something he had never done in his life before.

The accomplishment excited him. 'Hey, I've read a book!' he thought. 'I must tell someone.'

'I've got a book here,' he shouted to the guy in the next cell. 'Would you like to read it?'

'What's it called?'

'Hooked,' Eddie replied, hoping he was right.

'I've read it,' the guy said.

'What's the story about then?' Eddie asked, eager to check if he really had managed to read, but without letting the other guy know he couldn't. As the man went through the story Eddie realised it was exactly what he'd read. So he hadn't imagined it! He really *had* read a book!

Immediately he went and picked up the discarded *Journey Into Life* booklet and read it from cover to cover. On the last page he found an invitation to ask Jesus into his life. Without hesitation Eddie asked Jesus not once, but *six* times to come into his life and take over. He didn't know what he was expected to feel - if anything. But he actually felt nothing at all. No difference. So had anything happened?

Towards the end of his time in solitary the Governor came to Eddie's cell and said, 'I've been hearing good things about you, Murison. I think we'll put you back into circulation. Somehow I don't feel as if there's going to be any more hassle.'

Eddie felt suddenly confused. What was happening? He gathered his gear into a bundle to go back upstairs, but his head began to throb. He realised he really didn't want to go back to normal prison life with all the noise of banging doors and rattling keys. He'd grown to enjoy the quietness down here where he was free to think his own thoughts. Especially these last weeks.

As he packed up his last few bits and pieces he saw his bottle of medication: Largactil. It was what they gave him to keep him quiet and under control. 'I'm no' taking any more o' that rubbish,' he thought. 'That's doin' my box in.' And he threw it in the bin, feeling a quiet surge of inward strength as he did so.

'That's the best thing you've ever done,' commented the prison officer who was standing by. Together they went to Eddie's new cell on the ground floor. It was near enough to the Office so that the staff could keep an eye on him.

Next morning, after the normal breakfast time, he padded barefoot down to the canteen, clad only in pyjama bottoms, all of which was against the rules.

'Where's my breakfast?' he asked.

His old enemy, the cook, came right up to him. 'There's something different about you, Eddie. Your eyes aren't black any more.' Eddie knew he meant the hatred had gone from them. 'I'm not scared of you any more. I feel at peace with you.'

Now Eddie was the one who was scared! 'I must be getting soft,' he thought as he carried his breakfast back to his cell, totally confused. 'What's goin' on here?' he asked himself. 'That guy should be scared o' me. What's the problem? Something's happening. I'm gettin' soft.'

It was a few minutes before he realised: 'I asked Jesus into my life. So he *is* in. It must be him who has taken away the bitterness and anger and is making me soft.'

Then fear struck - it was no good being soft in prison. You never knew who would try to plunge you. He'd have to put up a front again ... pretend to be tough, like he was before. But inside he knew he was a different guy.

Before long he was living a different life quite openly. He started attending Bible studies and even getting men into his cell to read the Bible with him and talk about what it meant and what Jesus was doing in their lives from day to day. They used the Gideon Bibles which were around in the prison - maybe a few were nicked from the Chapel, but at least they were being read and studied. They prayed together as well, asking God to help them to get to know him better, to keep them safe and help them to talk about Jesus to any of the men who would listen. Not surprisingly they became known as the God Squad.

But Eddie didn't care what names he was called. Whenever he had the opportunity he would sit for hours reading his Bible and writing down what he felt God was saying to him. He grinned as he remembered how he'd always refused to write at school and now here he was, writing voluntarily! Ten o'clock came all too soon and the lights went out. But these days Eddie wasn't ready for bed so he would bang on the door.

'What do you want?' the officer in charge asked.

'Would you put the light back on please, Sir?' Eddie requested with an unaccustomed politeness which was little short of a miracle. 'I'm reading the Bible and doing a study. I need the light.'

And so his light would be burning until four or five o'clock in the morning. He just couldn't seem to get enough of it. First he read and then he wrote - he filled notebook after notebook with what he felt God was saying to him from the Bible. And then he would share these things with the other men who came to read with him.

All this happened at a time when many prisons were experiencing sudden outbreaks of violence, and it was rumoured that some of the inmates of Dumfries were to be transferred to a new prison at Shotts to make room for some of the troublemakers.

Eddie rather fancied a look at Shotts.

But it was not to be. Of the ten men who were Christians, nine were moved to Shotts. Eddie was sent to Glenochil. Under the same rearrangement scheme many of the hardest cases from Peterhead prison were being transferred to Glenochil, while men who were considered to need protection were being sent to Peterhead.

'What have I done wrong that I'm being sent to Glenochil?' Eddie wondered aloud in his prayers to God. 'I became a Christian, so why am I nae goin' wi' the others to Shotts? If I go to Glenochil I'm gonna end up being hard because I'm gonna have to look after mysel' and let them ken I'm nae softened up that much. I could lose my faith ....'

8

RELEASE

The thought that he might lose his faith really scared Eddie. He felt he'd only just found Jesus and he meant so much to him. But what would happen in a strange prison on his own? Could his faith stand the knocks it might have to take?

On his first day at Glenochil a man approached and started to make conversation. He was a quiet-looking, bearded man and Eddie was instantly wary. He decided to speak out boldly.

'Where's the Bible classes here?' he asked. He'd decided that making a stand at the start might help him hang on to his faith.

'You a Christian as well?' the man enquired.

'Are *you*?' Eddie countered, determined not to be the first to give anything away. Even when the man admitted he was, Eddie asked him a few salient questions just to be sure!

As they chatted, Eddie discovered that the man had been a police officer but he was serving six years for armed robbery. Which made him a prime target for the other inmates, Eddie realised. 'Maybe God has put me here to keep him safe,' he thought.

'Maybe I'm here to see that nobody damages him.'

At the first opportunity Eddie spoke up for his new found friend. 'Give this guy a break, will you?' he said. 'Leave him alone. He's done wrong, but so have we. He's a Christian and I'm a Christian. We both know that God can really help. So just leave him ... take the pressure off.'

Nobody spoke, but at least they knew now that the guy was not on his own. If anything happened to him, Eddie would be right in there as well. As a cop there would always be one or two who cold-shouldered him, but Eddie felt he had at least done what he could for his brother-in-Christ.

The two Christians soon found an unusual way to communicate with each other during the evenings. Each man would write what he was learning from God on a sheet of thin paper and, having obtained permission to go to the toilet, he'd slip the paper under the door of the other cell on the way.

One night as Eddie approached the door of the other man's cell, he heard him speaking aloud. But the sounds didn't sound like any language Eddie had ever heard.

'What's going on?' he wondered. 'Has this guy got something more than I've got?' He didn't like the thought at all.

Back in his cell he stormed at God: 'God, why have I nae got this? What's happenin'?'

He determined to find out more about it. At Glenochil Eddie had started to attend the meetings held by members of the Prison Fellowship, so on the next Sunday he spoke to one of the PF visitors, Eddie Macguire, about what he'd heard.

'How come he's speakin' in a funny language?' he demanded.

'What do you mean?' Macguire asked.

'He's sayin' things that's nae normal,' Eddie insisted.

Macguire suggested that the man might have been speaking in tongues, and went on to explain more about it to Eddie from the Bible. Then he changed the subject. 'How long have you got left to serve, Eddie?'

'Six weeks.'

'What are you going to do when you get out?' Macguire wanted to know.

'Don't know.' It had been one of his main preoccupations lately.

'How'd you like to come and stay with my family for a while when you get out?' Macguire offered.

'Yes, I would,' Eddie accepted gratefully. But later on he began to have doubts and even rang Macguire to decline the offer. Still later he phoned again and said he *would* like to come. It was all so confusing. Maybe if he could have a trial run ...?

So Eddie went to the Governor and asked if he could get out for a weekend to go and stay with a Christian family to see if he thought he could fit in there.

'Be sensible, Murison. You're doing time. You're not getting out.'

It was no use arguing so Eddie again phoned
Macguire to let him know the outcome. Macguire
understood. But then Eddie spoke to God. 'I'm nae
acceptin' this, Lord,' he said. 'I'm wantin' oot to see
if I'm gonna fit into this or no'.' He requested
another interview.

This time it was the Deputy Governor who saw
him. He made his request as before.

'Yes,' came the reply. 'I don't see why not.'

Eddie was stunned. As he stood there in shock the
Deputy Governor set out the terms.

'You'll get out on Sunday at ten o'clock in the
morning. You're to be back by twenty past four.'

When he knew he was going to be allowed out,
Eddie began to get ideas. If he could get hold of some
drugs while he was 'outside' and smuggle them back
in, he could make a tidy bit of money which could be
very useful when he was released. He spoke to one
or two inmates who could arrange for people to pass
the drugs over to him in Dollar, where he would be
staying for the weekend. But even as he made his
arrangements, Eddie was conscious that he wasn't
just planning to do wrong. He was intending to
commit a deliberate sin. The thought made him
unexpectedly uncomfortable ... guilty ... as if he had
a heavy burden right on top of his head.

In fact, once he actually arrived at the Macguire's
house, it was still bothering him and it completely
spoilt his appetite. Which was a pity because
Macguire's wife, Frankie, had specially prepared

his favourite meal - macaroni and cheese. But the thought of what he had agreed to do made Eddie feel as if he couldn't eat a bite.

He turned to Macguire. 'I've got to tell you,' he began. 'I'm here ... oot .. and I'm planning to take drugs back in. But I can't do it. I'm a Christian. I can't do that any more.'

Macguire nodded understandingly. 'Don't worry about it. It needn't go any further. If you really believe in God, he'll look after you. Just leave it at that.'

With that assurance Eddie's appetite returned and he did full justice to the macaroni. He thoroughly enjoyed the rest of the day with Eddie and Frankie Macguire and their three young daughters. It was great to have time to talk and laugh, and to see the way they lived as a family - so different from anything he had known before. They even prayed before they ate their meals! It all felt good to Eddie that day.

All too soon it was time to go back to prison and face the guys who were expecting the drugs he *hadn't* brought back. He knew it wouldn't be easy. Better have a word with the Lord.

'Well, Lord,' he prayed, 'My life could be in danger here because I'm involved in this deal with the drugs, and if I don't deliver I don't know what they'll do to me. And I can't even fight them,' he went on, 'cos I've only two weeks to go and there's no way I'm gonna get into trouble for fighting.'

On Monday morning on the way to the canteen Eddie saw two of the men sitting on the stairs, chatting to a third. They were all wearing shorts with a towel round their waists - and Eddie could guess why. They were out to plunge somebody! Dressed like that they could stab a guy, nip into the showers, wash all the blood off and disappear. Easy.

Eddie slipped into the toilets himself. He had a knife hidden away there for emergencies like this. But when he put his hand up to the hiding place, it came away empty. There was no knife! How could he defend himself if he had no knife? Would he just have to take whatever they did to him? He could always pray - but would it work? Could God really protect him? Then he remembered a fellow Christian from another Hall. At exercise time Eddie ran over to him.

'You've got to pray for me - my life's in danger here,' he said, and then explained about the drug episode.

'If it's gonna happen, you've just got to stand for it, Eddie,' the man said.

'I canna hit back I know, but ...'

'Tell them "Jesus loves you",' his friend suggested.

'I don't know if I can do that, man,' Eddie admitted. 'I don't think I'm there. I don't think I've that kind of faith.'

His faith was truly tested in the tense days that followed. He tried all he knew to find materials to make some sort of a knife, but it was impossible. He broke the leg of a chair, intending to try to fashion some sort of weapon, but then threw it down in disgust.

His paranoia made him barricade his door at night, yet still he didn't feel safe. He even told a prison officer that his life was in danger.

'Right, give us the names of the men who are threatening you,' the officer said.

'I'm nae gonna tell you names, but I've only got aboot a week left. Couldn't I be locked up by mysel' for a week?' Eddie appealed.

'Unless you tell us names, you're just going to have to go out there and face it,' the officer said.

'No way,' said Eddie. Locked in his cell that night Eddie appealed to God. 'Lord, I need you,' was all he said. But as he spoke the words, Eddie felt himself suddenly filled with peace, a total and complete peace, such as he had never experienced before. Next morning his door was opened at ten o'clock and the prison staff just disappeared. Eddie felt they guessed there was going to be a big fight and they just walked away.

But Eddie knew just what he was going to do. He went straight to the guy who intended to knife him, put his hand in and pulled the knife out of the man's waistband.

'Jesus doesna' want that,' he said. 'Jesus loves you.'

Eddie threw the knife down, and he could feel

love rising up inside him for the guy ... not his own love but the love of Jesus, flowing out. It was a strange, new feeling. It made him want to tell the other guy, and his mates, about what Jesus had for them.

A short time later the four men were sitting in Eddie's cell. Eddie sat with his back to the wall, still half-wondering why he hadn't used the knife on the guy ... what was really going to happen now that they were all together in a cell?

He sat there totally alert, his back straight, head down over his toes, poised for action. At the least movement he was going right in - head first. He would pulp the guy who made the wrong move. There was no way he was going to allow himself to be stabbed with only a week to go. But even as he sat there he could feel the love of God inside him. He began preaching to the men, sharing with them all the things he had been learning in Dumfries prison. Somehow the words were just spilling out of his lips.

'I'm a Christian. I believe in Jesus,' he told them. 'I don't want to go back into this kind of rubbish. I'm finished with this kinda life. And God can do the same for you if you open up and just listen to what I'm saying.'

But even as he heard the words tumbling from his mouth, part of Eddie's mind was wondering what the other guys must be thinking. Did they think he was some kind of a 'poofter' to be speaking about love? Part of him still didn't feel comfortable speaking about love to other men, but he did it anyway, letting the words rattle out of his mouth, almost as if he were not in control.

'Jesus loves you. He can help you. Crime's no' right ...'

Suddenly one of the guys interrupted him. 'Part o' me wants to walk out of the door, but the other part o' me wants to stay here.'

'Praise the Lord, man!' Eddie shouted. 'That shows that Jesus is here.'

An almost tangible peace filled the cell. All the fears and the paranoia and aggression had gone right out of the window. Eddie knew in a new way that Jesus was Lord of his life and in control of the situation. He found himself putting the word *love* in right, left and centre. He so much wanted them to know the love of God for themselves as he knew it. He had a beautiful sensation that he was being used ... that his fear had been replaced by power ... a power which was even reaching these guys!

The last few days passed uneventfully and suddenly the day of his release from prison arrived. He was sitting in the 'dub box', the tiny room where prisoners changed their clothes. All at once he was overcome by a rush of doubts.

'Is it right to go to Macguire's house?' he asked himself. 'Maybe I should go back to Aberdeen, hit the bevvie, get a woman and have a right carry on? Get some money...' The old way of life leered at him, with its own insidious invitation.

The next twenty minutes were the longest of Eddie's life as he waited for Macguire to collect him. The minutes seemed like hours. And as he waited an awful thought struck him.

'What if he doesna' show up?' he thought. 'I've only got a one way ticket to Dollar and if he doesna' come, I'm stuck.'

9

HIGHS AND LOWS

Macguire didn't let Eddie down. He arrived at the prison on time and took Eddie back to his home. Then began a lifestyle that was totally new.

Sometimes it seemed to Eddie that Jesus came into *everything*. Apart from Bible studies where he was used to reading about him, it seemed that whenever they turned on the radio there would be either a hymn like 'Jesus Loves Me', or something scriptural that seemed significant. Even on TV there would often be something coming through about God's love. And as if reflecting this, Eddie himself found he couldn't stop talking about Jesus and all that he had done for him.

To his surprise he discovered that his hosts were willing to spend hours talking - not only about Jesus, but also about his past life as they tried to help him sort things out.

He went along to their church and chalked up another new experience. When he heard people giving their testimony he whispered to Frankie: 'There's no way you'd get me speaking in church wi' all these folk.' But he surprised himself as he stood up shortly afterwards and shared what he felt about God and all the changes he was making in his life.

But after a while Eddie began to find this concentrated focus on Jesus was a bit over the top and getting on his nerves. He appealed to Macguire.

'Look me straight in the eyes and tell me - am I goin' daft? Am I goin' cuckoo?' he asked. 'I feel as if I'm ready for the nuthoose. I canna get away from it. I canna even close my eyes without thinking about Jesus. I canna even have twenty seconds to myself. It's all Jesus, Jesus, *Jesus!* When I look at anything all I see is what Jesus would see. I feel like I'm looking through Jesus' eyes. I feel I'm goin' cuckoo.'

Macguire shook his head. 'It's all right, Eddie,' he said gently. 'You're not going to go daft.'

But Eddie was not so sure. It was all so different and new and maybe this obsession with Jesus could land him in the 'nuthouse'. Then what would happen?

'Wait a minute. Let's just give it to God,' Macguire suggested.

Eddie was grateful, for his fear was very real. 'Lord,' he prayed, 'I hand up this fear of being daft and ending up cuckoo.'

In the following days the pressure lifted. He allowed himself to focus on other things besides the Bible and to achieve some kind of balance in his thinking. The Holy Spirit, who had revealed so much to him from God's Word, now began to show him how to settle down and learn to live.

And then one Thursday night Eddie appealed to the Macguires yet again. 'I feel I need prayer,' he said. 'I want to be filled with the Spirit.'

So the couple laid their hands gently on him and started to pray that the Holy Spirit would come upon Eddie. As they prayed Eddie started to feel shivery. He was aware of a tension inside him, but nothing seemed to happen. Nothing came through.

Eddie went off to bed disappointed. 'What's the score, God?' he prayed urgently. 'They prayed for me to be baptised, and I'm no' baptised. Why?'

Next morning when Eddie got up, Macguire was already away to his work but Frankie chatted to him as she made his breakfast. As usual the talk soon came round to Jesus. The old part of Eddie still felt it was a bit 'daft', but to the new Eddie, it felt good. Like the record Frankie put on before she went to get on with her housework.

At first Eddie was barely conscious of the words Marilyn Baker's soft voice was singing. But when he really started to listen, something inside him broke. 'Jesus, You are changing me, by your Spirit You're making me like You ...'.

Eddie leapt right off his chair, jumped over the coffee table, ran all through the house and coming back into the room he fell on his knees, tears coursing down his cheeks unstoppably. At the same time he felt as if something were pouring down all over him, sluicing out all the old stuff and filling him from the top of his head. It was as if he were being washed and made thoroughly *clean*, clean in a way he had never known before!

And still the tears came and he sobbed and sobbed. But he didn't care. He felt so light and free! And *clean!* 'Thank you, Lord,' he prayed. 'Oh, praise you, Jesus!'

When the record stopped Frankie came through to change it, and found Eddie still praising God through his tears.

'Oh, I'm sorry,' she said, 'I didn't know...'

'Forget it,' Eddie said. 'Come and pray with me.'

So they prayed together and Eddie told her what had just happened. Joyfully they gave thanks to God.

That night when he went to his room, Eddie started praying to God in tongues. At first it was like little wee noises, which Eddie couldn't understand at all, but he didn't mind. Somehow it just felt right to keep on praising God in that way and he kept on for hours. Next morning he shared the news with the delighted Macguires.

It took just two and a half weeks before crisis hit Eddie. He woke up one day and knew that he was totally confused. He was enjoying his new life and in one way he felt good, but in another he felt as if he no longer knew who he really was. He knew that God was changing him, filling him, washing him clean from what he'd been. But he also felt that God was asking him to give himself one hundred per cent to him. And that thought threw Eddie into confusion.

'I can't do it, God,' he groaned. 'I couldna give you a hundred per cent - I don't know how. I'm nae good enough.'

The spiritual change had been real all right. But he felt he just couldn't continue on that level. And that was when he told the Macguires a lie.

'I've got to go away tomorrow,' he said. 'I've been thinking about some money I stole and I want to give it back. I'll go and give it to the police in Aberdeen. I'll come back doon here after,' he promised.

It was a downright lie. The thoughts in his head were quite different.

'I'm wantin' to get awa' from here ... I'm just nae interested. I want to get oot.'

Maybe Eddie Macguire guessed these unspoken thoughts for he offered to go with Eddie. But Eddie refused.

'No, don't come with me. I want to do this on my own. I'll be all right,' he assured Macguire.

Eddie packed his few belongings together and next morning took the train to Aberdeen. Now he could get back to his old life. He would never be good enough to be a Christian anyway. So why keep trying?

But Eddie soon found that God was not as easy to run away from as Macguire had been. Walking along Aberdeen's main thoroughfare, Union Street, a few days later he happened to glance up a side street. The words *Abbey Christian Fellowship* caught his eye and somehow his feet followed. As if acting under remote control he entered the building and asked to speak to the pastor or whoever was in charge.

While waiting he wandered into the kitchen where two young women were making sandwiches. They offered him a cup of tea - and sandwiches to go with it. As he happily accepted these a tall, well-built man walked in.

'I'm Douglas MacIntyre,' the man said. 'Did you want to see me?'

Eddie introduced himself and soon they were seated in MacIntyre's small office. Without really understanding why, Eddie suddenly felt that he wanted to give Christianity another try.

'I'm a Christian,' he began, 'and I'm nae long out of prison. I've kinda run away from God. But now I'm staying up here and I'm looking for a church.'

'Fine,' said MacIntyre. 'Let's pray.'

After a few minutes Eddie changed into praying in tongues. He hoped the minister would guess he wanted him to lay hands on him. MacIntyre did, and he prayed against anything that would stop Eddie from following through on his new commitment.

So Eddie was back in a church - though he did not settle there easily. He was too mixed up inside himself for that. He still carried a load of guilt about his past life and just couldn't convince himself that he was good enough to be a Christian. On the other hand he resented some of the people who came to church - those who seemed to Eddie to have lots of money, live in big houses and have no problems. Eddie classed them all as snobs and felt more comfortable around the folk whom he felt were at his level - those who had been in prison.

It was a difficult time. He wanted to be in church and to worship Jesus, but he didn't feel he could trust anyone there, or open up to them. So how was he ever going to build up any relationships? Would he ever fit in there? Sunday by Sunday he sat there struggling with conflicting feelings - his need for fellowship and his lack of confidence in himself.

Then one Sunday morning Douglas MacIntyre preached from Acts, Chapter Twelve, where an angel touched the imprisoned Peter's side and his chains fell off and he was free. Eddie closed his eyes, thinking that Jesus had done exactly that for *him*. He had come into *his* prison and touched *him*, and set *him* free. He felt the tears starting to his eyes.

'Douglas.' He spoke the word, but the minister didn't hear him. So he said it again, louder this time. 'Douglas.'

Part of him knew that he didn't really need to ask permission to go up there, but another part of him was still tied up with the feeling that it was wrong to oppose authority. Douglas nodded to him.

'Is it all right if I share?' Eddie asked, tears streaming down his face and falling on to his pullover.

'Come on up,' MacIntyre invited.

So Eddie walked on to the platform and stood in front of the whole church, feeling no fear, just an overwhelming love.

'I've got love inside me,' he began. 'I just want to tell you that I love each and every one of you. I *love* you. And it's Jesus' love ... it's nae my love.'

He had had his say, and he came off the stage still weeping. From all over the church people spontaneously left their seats and clustered round Eddie. They shook his hand, grabbed his shoulder - even hugged him, mingling their tears of joy with his. Until that moment the hugs would have been a problem for Eddie, but now he hugged them back, even guys!

It was as if some great barrier in his life had come crashing down, broken to pieces. It was another new freedom - the freedom from the bondage of the fear of authority. For Eddie it was tremendous, another step forward to stability.

The freedom was tested shortly afterwards in an incident which Eddie found ironic.

He was coming out of church one morning with his Bible under his arm when a CID car came round the corner. He felt the men inside the car looking at him and anger seemed to roar to life inside him. Instantly he recognised that he shouldn't have such a wrong attitude towards the police now that he was a Christian, so he sent up a quick prayer.

'Lord, I didna mean that.'

The car stopped. 'Do you want a lift?' the officers asked.

Eddie was overwhelmed - he felt he couldn't handle such a swift answer to his prayer! But nevertheless he accepted their offer and the CID drove him to his Mum's house. On the way Eddie eagerly shared with the officers what Jesus had been doing in his life.

'God has really changed me,' Eddie assured them. 'I'm a different guy. And Jesus loves you too ....'

'Awa' ye go!' one of the officers responded, 'we've had too much of you.' But the other policeman seemed to accept what he said.

Why then did Eddie hit the bottle at that stage? What made him start drinking whisky and go back to his old way of life? Why did he turn his back on the church - and on God - for the next few months? He stopped living at his mother's house and moved into a mobile home, and even though men from the church came and visited him there to say they were missing him from the fellowship, it didn't change things. He had been seeing a Christian girl, but now he decided to finish with her too. Once again his life was going rapidly downhill.

One night he and his brother were in a pub when a hefty, bouncer type of man started making advances to his brother's girlfriend.

'I'm gonna plant you in two minutes,' Eddie thought. He shifted the table a fraction and got himself into position - ready for action. Meanwhile his brother was looking at Eddie, mutely appealing for his help. Eddie nodded an acknowledgement and spoke to the other man.

'Get your hands off her,' he ordered. 'Ootside.'

Eddie had no intention of fighting in front of witnesses. The two men hustled down the stairs and round to the back of the pub. To his disgust the man took off his jacket and Eddie tore into him in the old style. Wham! Splatter! He must have hit him about four times before he went down on the deck.

Then Eddie started kicking him. He was about to leave him when he saw a big aluminium barrel. Here was a chance to really hurt the guy! He lifted it up above his head and then threw it with all his weight. The missile hit its mark and the man gave a loud grunting sound - UUGGHH!

'To pot wi' you,' the unrepentant Eddie said as he picked up the guy's discarded jacket and threw it on a nearby roof. No need to leave evidence lying around.

He went back home. But this was not like the old days. The memory of what he had just done began to exert a fierce and unrelenting pressure. He was totally disgusted with himself.

In the end he went down on his knees. 'Jesus,' he prayed, 'I really repent and ask for forgiveness.'

His repentance lasted until next morning when he picked up more drink. That night he carried on drinking and got into a fight with some hard men in

Aberdeen. He finished up with a black eye, bleeding nose and bloody knuckles.

In the drink sodden recesses of his brain, Eddie knew he had to get help. He had to find somebody who would listen ... who would understand about the state he was in.

Two o'clock in the morning found him staggering up to the door of a manse. He rang the bell and waited.

Alan Sharp, the minister, answered the door.

Swaying unsteadily, Eddie made his plea. 'I need help,' he muttered. 'I've got a drink problem.'

'Right. Come back in the morning and I'll see you,' said Sharp.

'You'll see me now,' Eddie insisted. 'If you've got the love of God in you, you'll see me right now!'

10

REACHING OUT

The minister eventually managed to persuade Eddie to go home and promised to come and see him next day. He was as good as his word.

'Do you still want help?' he enquired when he called on Eddie the following afternoon.

'Yes.' Eddie felt it had to be now or never.

'Well, I've phoned a place in Fyvie,' Sharp said. 'It's a Centre for Alcoholics and they're willing to take you in. Pack your gear.'

Eddie obeyed, wondering what sort of a place he'd be going to now. Sunnybrae Centre was set in the midst of attractive countryside near Fyvie in Aberdeenshire. A large, low building housed the living accommodation which comprised a lounge, toilet facilities and fourteen single rooms, with a games room and staff housing situated nearby.

At first Eddie wondered how he would manage to cope with living way out in the country. It was the silence that bothered him most. It seemed really eerie. But he found the first few days were full of a variety of activities. Counselling sessions and Bible studies were interspersed with weightlifting and games of pool.

115

He became acquainted with Norman, who was in charge of the Centre, and his colleague, Ronnie. Both men were especially keen that Eddie should give the place a chance, and not quit prematurely.

On the Saturday after he arrived Eddie was encouraged to go to a Conference on evangelism in nearby Inverurie. During the weekend he attended various workshops and then decided to go to the prayer session on the Sunday morning. At that meeting the leader suggested that if anyone wanted to come forward for prayer, they should do so.

Eddie knew he must respond, though he felt he had no need to actually go forward. Hadn't he already made a commitment to the Lord? Surely that was enough? So he stayed in his seat as he made his prayer.

'Lord, I need help with drink, but I'm nae gonna work for it. I canna. I made a commitment in jail in front of people, but you'll have to do this for me. If you do, I'll never walk away from you again.'

He returned to Fyvie that afternoon with a renewed interest in Christian things. Once in his room, he took out his Bible. It seemed to fall open at the fifty-first chapter of Isaiah and the words of verse twenty-two leapt out at him.

'This is what your Sovereign Lord says, your God, who defends his people. "See, I have taken out of your hand the cup that made you stagger, from that cup ... you *will never drink again.*" '

The Word came to him with such power that

Eddie knew within himself that he had been healed, set completely free from alcohol! Jesus had answered the prayer he had prayed at Fyvie! It was an amazing feeling. He praised the Lord for it. Just an hour or two later friends called to see him.

'I'm coming hame wi' you,' Eddie declared. 'I feel fine. God's dealt wi' me.'

Norman tried to dissuade him. 'You've only been here a few days, Eddie. Don't run away.'

'But I'm OK,' Eddie insisted. 'Jesus has healed me of drink. I want to go back home.'

Not without some misgivings on the part of the staff, Eddie was, in fact, allowed to leave the Centre with his visitors. No-one could have known then that the word Eddie had received from Isaiah would prove to be a truly prophetic word. From that day to the time of writing, five years later, he has never drunk alcohol.

The freedom from dependence on alcohol had an unexpected effect on Eddie. He began to feel a deep concern for alcoholics and the people who lived on the streets of Aberdeen. It was as if something was growing inside him, something he would never have thought possible, a love for hurting people and a determination that something should be done to help them. But he had no idea how to set about it. Then one day he was standing in church, drinking tea with Douglas, the pastor and another member called Archie. Maybe he could share his concern with them?

'What's the church doing for the folk outside?'
he challenged, nodding towards the long, clear glass
windows which overlooked the passing parade of
people and traffic in Union Street below. 'There's all
these folk and a lot of them are in real need, but what
is the Church doing aboot it?'

He raged on for quite a while in the same vein,
unable to contain the confusion and anger he felt,
letting it all spill out. To him the need was so
obvious. Surely the Church should be doing something about it?

He was still frustrated when he left the two men
and he mulled over it for the rest of the day. In the
evening he went and apologised to them for some of
the strong language he had used. 'What you said was
right enough, Eddie,' they admitted. 'It was your
attitude that was wrong.' He still had so much to
learn!

But the urge to do something would not leave
Eddie. Yet what *could* he do? He was only one man,
and not a rich one at that. But if it was God who was
putting this concern into his heart, surely God would
show him the next step?

So Eddie turned expectantly to his Bible. And
there, in Isaiah, Chapter 49, he found words which
seemed like a direct command from the Lord. '..say
to the captives, "Come out," and to those in darkness, "Be free!" They will feed beside the roads and
find pasture on every barren hill. They will neither
hunger nor thirst. He who has compassion on them

will guide them and lead them beside springs of water.'

As he read the words over and over, meditating on them, Eddie knew deep inside him that God wanted *him* to go and feed the people who were living on the streets, and preach the Word of God to them. It seemed to him that the 'springs of water' was a word picture of Jesus flowing through him to the needy people of Aberdeen.

But how could he possibly put it into practice?

He started small by making a few flasks of soup and trekking round the streets where he knew people dossed down for the night. He found them in bushes, boxes, doorways or stretched out on the back seats of buses which were parked for the night. Others were in derelict houses, on benches in Stewart Park or just sleeping out on the beach.

Eddie would gently shake a sleeping figure and say: 'Jesus loves you. Would you like some hot soup?' Then as the man supped the warming liquid, Eddie would encourage him to talk and share his problems. 'Let's pray about this,' Eddie would say, before moving on to search out the next needy person.

Quite soon Eddie was an accepted and most welcome visitor, especially when he started bringing blankets along with the soup. He got some of these from his Mum and some from the Salvation Army - in fact, once word got around, it was surprising how people chipped in to help, although much of

his own 'dole' money still went on soup. People
donated Bibles, and Thermos flasks arrived from as
far away as Perth! Whatever the need, God seemed
to provide through his people.

But the more God provided, the more hurting
people Eddie seemed to find! As the weeks went by
he continued to contact homeless people, prosti-
tutes, homosexuals, glue sniffers, as well as alcoholics and people who had been sexually abused. Their
problems were infinitely varied, but Eddie knew
there was one answer to them all - the love of Jesus.
This was the theme of all his conversations with
them.

Around eight o'clock one morning Eddie was
tramping home with his big bags of empty flasks
when he met the pastor and an elder of the church.
They could not have failed to realise what Eddie had
been doing. Shortly after this encounter he was
given permission to use the Abbey Fellowship's
kitchen premises to cook his soup.

Then, unexpectedly, a co-worker materialised.
Don Robertson, ex-con and drug offender, came to
Aberdeen from England, feeling it was where the
Lord wanted him to be. Like Eddie, he had been
saved while serving a prison sentence, so he under-
stood the problems the street folk were facing and he
offered his help. After praying about it together,
Eddie and he started working together.

From these small beginnings a scheme called
OFTAN developed. 'Outreach For The Aberdeen

Needy' was based in the Abbey Fellowship premises. At first their hall became a store for the blankets
and used clothing which people donated. Eddie still
went out on foot with his flasks of soup, but he
started bringing some people back to the church for
breakfast, a wash and shave, and even a change of
clothes when necessary.

Soon the church started to keep its doors open
most of the day, serving simple meals to those who
came, meals provided by God as he prompted his
people to send gifts.

One day the inevitable happened. Sixty people
were in the hall, hoping for a meal, and there was no
food to give them. So Eddie and Don did the most
practical thing they could think of - they prayed,
reminding God of their need.

Half an hour later a lorry drew up and delivered
six hundred cans of Crosse & Blackwell's soup!
Then someone arrived with loaves of bread and
another brought butter! It was only a simple meal,
but it tasted like a feast. And when Eddie preached
to the folk that day, he preached 'on a high', elated
by God's wonderful answer to their prayer.

Through OFTAN, Eddie didn't aim just to meet
people's material needs. He wanted to offer them the
Bread of Life, and the Living Water - Jesus. So as
people sat informally round the tables after a meal,
Eddie or Don would talk to them simply about God
and share his word with them. Sometimes someone
would bring a guitar and sing songs which also told

the Good News about Jesus and his love for outcasts
and strangers.

Eventually some of them did receive Christ into
their lives; others were healed in answer to prayer.
Eddie could sense God really working in people's
lives ... changing them completely.

And Eddie knew that God was changing *him* too.
Slowly but surely the old quick-tempered, self-
centred Eddie was being moulded into a different
person. As he'd read in the Bible, in Christ he was a
new person. The old Eddie was a thing of the past. It
was great to feel it and to try to live it out day by day.

One thing which would help that would be a place
of his own - a flat where he could be independent and
perhaps even use it to help other people. Hearing of
one which might be suitable, he went to see the
solicitor concerned. 'I'm interested in the flat you
have for renting,' he said boldly, conscious that the
deposit was likely to be £200 and the only money he
had was a Social Security Giro for £50'. 'Right,' said
the solicitor. 'If you can give me £50 for a deposit,
the flat's yours.'

'Hallelujah, man!' said Eddie to the somewhat
surprised solicitor, as he chalked up yet another
answered prayer.

His joy was increased when he received a gift of
£50 the same day towards his OFTAN work! God
was really encouraging him!

From the start the flat was open house to all
comers. Even when he was out, Eddie left a key

under the mat so that people could come in and use the place like home. They could have a shower, make a meal, cook what they wanted, watch TV or videos on the brand new colour TV he had been given.

Nothing was ever stolen - in fact he soon found that people were actually bringing in more food than they ate! It was an amazing time of learning more about God's ability and willingness to provide, in our own times.

Eddie was learning to behave differently too. No longer did he barge through life, intent only on what *he* wanted. Instead he tried to consider the other person's point of view. He was even losing his fear of people from a different social background, and learning how to handle all his relationships better. Which was just as well, for an important new relationship was right around the corner!

Two of his pals asked him to go with them to the YMCA. Usually he would have been glad enough to go, but on that particular night he felt a strange reluctance. Nevertheless he *did* go and found the usual crowd of older teenagers hanging around. Maureen, an attractive, dark-haired young woman from Orkney, was doing her best to talk to the lads about Jesus, but they were giving her a rough time with their jeers and rude remarks. 'Agh! Jesus is just a heap o' rubbish ...' one young lad sneered.

He'd heard similar remarks often enough before, but this one caught Eddie on the raw. Maybe it

wasn't his place, but he felt he *had* to say something.
'Look - shut up!' he ordered. 'I've been in prison an'
I know God's real.' Attention was riveted on Eddie
as he told them about his past life and how God had
met him in prison and changed him completely. The
lads listened because Eddie was one of them - he
knew the score.

When he'd finished it was time to set off on his
soup round. He reckoned there were plenty of Christians in the YM to carry on talking to the young folk.
He'd better be on his way.

As he went out of the door, a young woman was
walking in. Eddie's response was automatic, and
favourable. 'She's nae a bad bit o' stuff,' he thought
approvingly. And then went on his way to hand out
soup.

But he returned to the YM the next night. And the
next. He discovered that the girl's name was Leslie.
When she asked if he would give his testimony again
to more of the lads, he agreed.

'I'd like to hear it myself,' Leslie said. Eddie was
encouraged. Further acquaintance had confirmed
his first opinion and he was definitely interested in
pursuing *this* relationship. Eddie eventually started
helping with some of the YM clubs on a regular
basis, playing football with the lads, giving short
talks, or just sitting chatting, trying to get the kids to
open up a bit about their problems. And he soon
learned that they had real problems, for some of
them came from very unhelpful home backgrounds.

One night Leslie offered Eddie a lift home in her car. On the way they called in at her flat for a coffee. Then they decided to have a time of prayer together. Sitting one on each side of the coffee table, they began to pray.

Without any warning a thought came to Eddie as he sat there with closed eyes. 'Look to your right and see your wife.' He dismissed the thought as crazy at once. Leslie was the only other person there and she was sitting *opposite him*. There *was* no-one on his right! But when Leslie started to pray he realised that she had moved to kneel beside him on the floor - on his right! Unnerved, he got to his feet and moved away. Leslie opened her eyes, wondering what was happening. She too moved away. They stared at each other across the space.

Eddie's thoughts were running riot. 'What's happenin'? I'm no' interested. I'm wantin' Jesus. I'm nae wantin' a woman. I've just come through a divorce - the papers'll be here any day. Why all this?' Tense and shaking at the same time, he wondered how he was going to explain himself to the bewildered Leslie.

'What is it?' she asked, unsure of what might happen next.

Eddie felt he had to tell her. 'I feel God's saying that you're going to be my wife.' Maybe it sounded stupid, but it was the truth.

As they parted shortly afterwards Eddie was convinced she must think he was off his head!

The next night he was standing outside her flat, waiting, when she drove round the corner in her old banger of a car. After a coffee they decided to go for a walk on the beach. This time there were no awkward feelings, both knew their friends were praying for them. There, as they walked together on the shore, their relationship moved into a new dimension of warmth and closeness. With God's help this would be a lasting relationship of real love.

It was not without its early pinpricks of misunderstanding, as when Leslie would refuse to hold Eddie's hand while walking down the street together. Their relationship was so new that Leslie wanted to keep it private for a little while longer. But Eddie was convinced that she was just ashamed to be seen walking hand in hand with an ex-con. His old fear of being thought inferior tormented him again.

Shortly afterwards they became engaged. Eddie shared this exciting piece of news with some young people at an Aberdeen school, when he was asked to give his testimony at one of their lunchtime Scripture Union meetings. After telling the teenagers about his early life and many prison sentences, he shared how Jesus had saved him and given him a completely new lifestyle. 'God even told me who my wife was to be, and we're going to get married soon. We believe the Lord will provide all we need. I'm unemployed right now but God is really wonderful. You'd better believe it.'

That night Eddie's phone rang. It was the SU

leader from the school he had visited, and he had exciting news for Eddie - another unexpected answer to prayer.

'My mother died not long ago,' the man began, 'and she left an engagement ring. I feel the Lord is saying that it would be right for me to give it to you for Leslie.'

An elated Eddie rushed to share the news with his fiancée. At first she was unsure at the thought of having an old ring, one she hadn't helped to choose. Maybe she wouldn't even like it.

In the event the 'old' ring proved to be a beautiful design of platinum and diamonds. God was giving them something they could never have afforded. What was more, it was the first real ring Eddie had ever offered to a girl.

And it was a perfect fit!

11

ROUGH ROADS

Eddie and Leslie were married on the 25th August
1989 in Gerrard Street Baptist Church, Aberdeen,
where Leslie was a member. Her own Pastor, Alistair
Brown, performed the ceremony and Eddie's Pastor, Douglas MacIntyre, was his best man.

After the ceremony they drove away in a Rolls
Royce to the reception at the Grampian Bus Social
Club, refreshing themselves on the way with
Appletize at Eddie's request, instead of the cham-
pagne which was normally supplied. The whole
affair was a happy occasion with much banter and
even a practical joke or two! They flew off to
Portugal on a honeymoon which not even sunstroke
and sunburnt lips could spoil!

Back in Aberdeen a few weeks later, Eddie took
up the new job which had been confirmed just the
day before their wedding. On that day Eddie had
gone to the Pastor to share what he believed to be a
word of knowledge from the Bible. In 1 Corinthians,
Chapter Nine and verse fourteen Eddie had read: '...
the Lord has commanded that those who preach the
gospel should receive their living from the gospel.'

As a result, on the day of their wedding, the Abbey Fellowship confirmed that, since he was to preach God's Word, they would start to pay Eddie a wage as he continued the work of OFTAN. This was a relief to the young couple in more ways than one, and it gave Eddie some interesting news to share with the man in the Employment Centre.

During the preceding months this official and Eddie had had many verbal exchanges. Reasonably enough the Employment officer had been insisting that Eddie try to find work. Eddie's replies must have been hard for him to fathom.

'I'm here in Aberdeen because Jesus has sent me here,' Eddie claimed. 'In one way I *am* working full-time, and I'm going to be called into full-time ministry, so please lay off the pressure on me because God has got a job for me. If you gi'e me a job it's no' gonna be right,' he went on. 'God will find me a job here, wait and see.'

They *had* waited and incredibly, Eddie's giros had never been stopped. Perhaps it was because one day the officer had taken Eddie into a private room, where Eddie had explained how he'd been in prison, and God had changed him, and had special plans for him - plans for full-time work. Eddie had gone on to share the gospel with him and the man had listened. After that there had been no further pressure on Eddie from that source.

So it was great to be able to go and tell the officer that at last he had a job as a full-time evangelist and would no longer be needing Social Security money.

'God's answered your prayer then,' was the man's comment.

'No,' said Eddie. 'He's just carrying out his plans for my life, because that's what he's chosen for me to do.'

Eddie and Leslie started their married life living in Leslie's small but comfortable flat - with Benjie. Even before they married, both Eddie and Leslie felt quite strongly that they would need a dog to complete their home, so they decided to get one right away. The trouble was that Eddie wanted a German Shepherd and Leslie preferred a Bearded Collie. The situation was at stalemate until one evening Leslie went to buy a Chinese carry-out. While he was waiting for her outside the shop, Eddie slipped across the road to buy a paper. As soon as he opened it the first thing that caught his eye was an advertisement: Bearded Collies for sale. Price £70.

Eddie eagerly showed Leslie the advert, remembering that he'd received a gift of £40 just that day. They'd agreed earlier to go halves, and he already had *his* half. Maybe this would be the right dog for them? That same evening they went to the kennels. Leslie found it hard to choose, but when a brown and white puppy came snuffling round Eddie's ankles, it seemed *he* had chosen *them*!

At first Benjie was so small that he fitted easily into Eddie's pocket. In fact Eddie often carried him there when he went out working on the streets, because Benjie was very clever at sniffing out people who might be sleeping deep in the bushes. He made Eddie's job quite a bit easier.

The months slipped by, and for almost a year their marriage seemed to be going well enough. But at that point, things started to go dreadfully wrong.

At first neither of them understood what was happening, but Eddie's insecurity began to surface more and more often, always in unacceptable ways. Deep down he was grateful for all that he had - a lovely Christian wife, a nice home, Benjie and work that he enjoyed. He knew that the Lord had given him more than he ever dared hope for, so why should he feel so insecure? Why was this fear lurking deep inside him, that he might one day lose it all as he had lost so much all through his life?

This fear, which he never dared articulate even to himself, sometimes drove him to unreasonable behaviour and threatened to destroy everything he had worked so hard to achieve. It wasn't that he didn't love Leslie. He did. But it was such a possessive love that it was slowly squeezing the life out of her love for him.

Few marriages run smoothly from day one, but people who have seen a good marriage in action have a far better chance of making their own marriage work. Eddie's early memories did nothing to help and he was painfully conscious that his two earlier attempts at marriage had failed miserably. Would he ever learn to cope?

Leslie was also confused. Coming from a happy family background, she found it hard to understand Eddie's insecurity and what seemed like constant demands for attention and affection. Before starting work at the Aberdeen YMCA, she had worked in offices, and had also been a professional ice skater. Her great love was travel, and it was while she was visiting Holland in 1982 that she stayed at a Christian Youth Hostel and, as a result, became a Christian herself.

After that, office work lost its appeal, though it was a necessary source of income. Shortly after she returned from Holland she took a job in a sport and recreation office and was encouraged to qualify as a sports coach. That qualification helped her to get into Jordanhill College in Glasgow, where she studied for a Youth and Community Education Diploma from 1984 to 1986. Once qualified she looked around for a Christian opening and took a job with the YMCA in Strathclyde. After a year she moved to the YMCA at Aberdeen where the main emphasis was on youth work.

She had been working in Aberdeen for three years when Eddie appeared on the scene. He called in to the YMCA before setting out on his nightly soup-round. Leslie had already heard something of his story from a colleague, so although they were only introduced briefly that evening, it was a significant meeting.

Maybe she should have guessed from the definite

twinkle in his eye that theirs would be a whirlwind
courtship, and that Eddie would be eager to get
married as soon as possible, though Leslie would
have preferred to take things at a slower pace. He had
told her about his past life - his marriages and
children, his times in prison - but they also spent
quite a lot of time reading the Bible and praying
together, asking God to show them the way forward.

As far as Leslie could see, the trouble was that
almost everything they read in the Bible seemed to
relate to marriage in one way or another. Jeremiah
29:4-6 was especially clear. 'This is what the Lord ...
says: Build houses and settle down .... Marry and
have sons and daughters.' Hadn't Eddie even prayed
for an engagement ring and the Lord had provided
one!

Leslie's parents were understandably cautious,
and certainly not enthusiastic about their marriage.
But, after a ten months courtship, in spite of all the
difficulties, they had married.

Leslie continued to work at the YMCA, though
she found her work was now constantly interrupted
as Eddie either phoned or dropped in for coffee. She
began to find it hard to cope with - after all, she was
in charge at the YMCA and had a job of work to do.
And Eddie's reasons for calling were often seeming-
ly trivial - he was missing her, or he wondered if she
still loved him!

He seemed to hate her going out to work at the
YMCA in the evenings, and sometimes he'd pick a

quarrel and make her late. If she occasionally wanted to go out with a few girlfriends, he would think it was because she didn't want to spend time with him. Even in church he resented her speaking to any men, accusing her of 'fancying' them.

Inevitably, the growing possessiveness, suspicion and irrational behaviour caused tensions to build up between them which usually resulted in verbal abuse. Eddie reacted in the only way he knew how - shouting and accusing his wife of all kinds of things which were quite untrue. Eddie could keep up such abuse for long periods as his suspicions and fears fuelled each outburst. 'Surely this wasn't the way marriage was supposed to be?' Leslie thought in despair. She became tense and nervous, never knowing when the next outburst would come. If only something could be done to help Eddie!

Douglas MacIntyre was having similar thoughts. Eddie had called on him for help when he found he had relapsed into his old habit of swearing, but Douglas suspected that the swearing was just a symptom of a much deeper problem. They had talked and prayed together, but in spite of countless hours of listening to Eddie and trying to get through to him over a period of many months, nothing seemed to make any difference. Maybe if he could go and stay at a counselling centre somewhere, they might be able to help.

Douglas 'phoned around and managed to arrange for Eddie to spend a weekend at Ellel Grange, a well-appointed country house near Lancaster where a variety of Christian Healing and Counselling Courses are held. It meant that both he and Leslie would have to be there with Eddie, but he was prepared for this if it would help.

Shortly afterwards the three travelled down to Lancashire, hoping for a real breakthrough. On arrival they were assigned a set of trained counsellors who ministered to them during the weekend. Leslie's hopes were raised several times as Eddie seemed to go along with all that the counsellors said during a session, but they were swiftly dashed when, within the hour, Eddie retracted on everything.

On Sunday they travelled home, knowing that nothing in the whole weekend had got through to Eddie. So where did they go from here?

Douglas next managed to find a place on the West Coast of Scotland where Eddie could go to stay with a Christian couple and receive counselling from Roseanne. Again, Leslie hoped that there might be a positive outcome.

Eddie arrived there one evening and his counselling was to begin the following day. But even during that first evening Roseanne suspected that Eddie was not telling her the truth. She rang to check with Leslie. Sure enough, Eddie was lying to her much as he had lied to Douglas.

'He obviously has a lying spirit,' she told Leslie. 'We'll have to deal with it.'

Confronted with the truth and after prayer, a

measure of healing came to Eddie. Unfortunately, before any more work could be done with him, Roseanne's mother died and she was called away to Glasgow. Eddie returned to Aberdeen, where Douglas again took over the task of trying to sort him out.

One afternoon Leslie was ironing some shirts and Eddie was sitting watching TV. Casually, and without really thinking, Leslie asked how one of the alcoholics was doing. Eddie leapt up from the couch, knocking the iron down on the floor beside her. 'Why are you asking about him?' he shouted. 'Do you fancy him or something? Maybe you should have married *him*!'

Leslie was horrified, totally unable to understand her Jekyll and Hyde character of a husband. The folk in OFTAN really respected him, she knew, because he was so helpful to everyone and even counselled people with problems sometimes. But at home it was quite another story!

One night the torrent of abuse was more than she could bear, so after trying in vain to reason with him, she fled to their bedroom and began to sob uncontrollably. She must have cried for almost two hours, by which time Eddie had calmed down and apologised as he often had in the past. But this time it was as if something inside her had broken and the tears just wouldn't stop.

Infuriated because she wouldn't speak to him, Eddie started to shout again, as if it were the only way he knew to control the situation. Leslie simply lay there sobbing, feeling weak and completely drained. She wanted only to die.

Things had been bad before, but always Leslie had come round and accepted his apologies. They'd made it up. But the constant crying unnerved Eddie. In desperation he 'phoned his minister friend, Douglas MacIntyre, who came round right away.

Eddie explained what had happened, admitting that such things had been going on for quite some time. Douglas promised counselling help for both of them, and also suggested that Eddie should withdraw from OFTAN. His way of living was just not in line with what he preached to the men there.

This was a hard blow to Eddie, for he loved his work and really felt the Lord had given it to him. Unfortunately in his disturbed state he saw his dismissal as being Leslie's fault. He even began to put pressure on her to leave the YMCA.

The hassles and wild outbursts continued, in spite of the fact that Douglas spent many hours counselling Eddie, trying to help him sort himself out. But Eddie could not cope with the challenges Douglas gave him and he continued to try to lie his way out of each situation.

One night Eddie again spewed out a load of accusations against Leslie, and then stormed out of the house, saying that he might not be back. Leslie had heard it all before and guessed he'd soon reappear, but before he did she rang Douglas and asked him to come round to the house. No-one had seen

Eddie in full fling and Leslie often wondered if they even believed her accounts.

It wasn't long before Eddie reappeared and just the fact of Douglas' presence made him instantly suspicious. He started to wind himself up, saying all the usual stupid things. Douglas tried to calm him down but it was no use, Eddie stormed on violently and finally grabbed a knife and threatened to kill himself right there in front of them!

Douglas did finally manage to get Eddie quietened down, but Leslie had had enough. She insisted that he leave there and then.

'I think we should separate for at least two months until you get some more counselling help,' she said. 'Then, if you really *do* change, we'll see ...'.

12

TOWARDS THE FUTURE

Eddie moved in with his mother yet again. Leslie stayed on in their flat and continued to attend the Abbey Fellowship, while Eddie began to worship at a Brethren Assembly. As far as their marriage was concerned the future looked bleak indeed.

It was a dark time of the year - Christmas was approaching and this in itself filled Eddie with dread. He remembered all too clearly the Christmas Day when he'd received the fateful letter while he was in prison. What awful thing might happen this Christmas?

Black thoughts filled Eddie's mind - what was the good of going on with God? He had saved him in prison, but if he couldn't save his marriage, what kind of a God was he? Was there any good going on with him, or even with life?

Leslie's feeling was mostly one of relief. Eddie still made a pest of himself by phoning or coming to the flat, always wanting reassurance that the separation was only temporary and that she'd still be around when he got himself sorted out. She began to find his persistence wearing, and whereas she had once been afraid of what Eddie might do, now her fear was turning to anger that he wasn't, in fact, staying away and giving her peace. 'I want nothing to do with you,' she told him angrily, on more than one occasion. 'I don't know if I'll be here or not. Leave me alone!'

She knew he was supposed to be getting counselling, but she could see no difference in him and until she did, she just didn't want to know him. The hurt was too raw.

At that point Mike and Jan Wendes began to counsel Eddie. This young couple led a house group Bible study in Aberdeen and they were more than willing to help Douglas minister to Eddie. Douglas was the first man to have won Eddie's trust, and it was this one good experience that helped him to open up to Mike and Jan. The fact that Jan herself had suffered some of the same rejections as Eddie, gave him confidence in her. He sensed that at least she knew something of what he was feeling. Little by little Eddie was able to share with them the deep hurts of his past life and as the bitterness spilled out, prayer enabled healing to flow in its place.

For so long Eddie had not been a trustworthy person himself and this very fact made it incredibly difficult for him to trust other people. He had also found it hard to respond properly to authority. His instinct was always to resist any attempt at direction, and this made any counselling difficult. But as the weeks and months went by, more of the hard, violent parts of Eddie gradually fell away, and a calmer, more sensitive personality emerged.

Their next aim was to try to see if they could bring the unfortunate couple back together again. It was not an easy process! They started by inviting Leslie to make a foursome for a game of badminton. Leslie was willing to play badminton, but not with Eddie.

'You know, we really feel Eddie is responding to our help,' they reassured her. 'He *is* changing.' But Leslie couldn't see it. At that point she just was not ready to give it a try. Some time later the Wendes' invited Leslie to their home when Eddie was there too. Leslie went, but inside she still felt hard and angry and ended up in tears. She still could not consider reconciliation. At that time the Wendes' were not suggesting that Eddie and Leslie should start living together again; they just wanted them to be friends. But Leslie was adamant.

The truth was that Leslie herself was needing counselling help. She needed to pour out how she was feeling about the whole situation to someone who would know how to answer the questions which were tormenting her.

'Where is God in all this?' she asked herself. Had she been wrong to marry Eddie? She had thought she was following God's guidance, so why was all this happening?

'I never had all this bother before I became a Christian,' she stormed inwardly. 'But even as a Christian I was happy in my work at the YMCA. It's only since I got married that everything is falling apart.'

She recalled the good relationship she used to have with God - now she didn't even know if he was there or not. She couldn't hear his voice like she used to. She couldn't even pray. She was going through all the motions at work and attending church, but it was just an empty sham. She didn't feel she had a relationship with God at all.

Deep down she blamed God for the hurt she had suffered. In putting up barriers against Eddie so that she wouldn't be hurt again, she seemed somehow to have shut God out too! It was one horrible situation and it made her weep - often.

Then one day a friend handed her a book: *From Prison to Praise* by Merlin Carothers. In it the author urged people to praise God in all circumstances.

'Right - I'll try it!' Leslie decided, though without much hope. So she started to praise God for her situation. She didn't mean a word of what she was saying, but somehow, as she went on reading her way through the book night after night and praising God afterwards, some of the barriers she had erected gradually came down. It was a slow process, but it did work. For Leslie, it was the turning point.

At last she was able to admit that her anger and bitterness was actually hurting *her* even more than Eddie. Together with a friend she prayed over all these hurting areas in her life during the next few days, and at long last she began to feel better inside. No longer bitter and tense with anger, but more at peace and perhaps even willing to think about seeing Eddie again.

Learning to trust him again was not easy. He had made so many empty promises in the past, dare she have any confidence in him now? Cautiously she continued to meet Eddie, at first only in the company of Mike and Jan. She had to admit that he did seem to be calmer and more considerate, but was it for real? Only time would tell.

She started to pick Eddie up from his mother's house each week and drive him to Mike and Jan's home. There they had long talks about how they were both feeling and then they would pray together with Mike and Jan. Eventually they were able to sit beside each other again - even to hold hands! And in the end Leslie agreed to take Eddie back to live in their home again. With God's help, healing was under way and the five-month separation was over.

It was not the end of their problems, but now at least they knew where to turn if ever things even started to go wrong. They had learned they were not on their own but that other members of the Christian family were always willing to do all they could to help. Fortunately there were several people in the Abbey Fellowship at that time who could be called on, and during the troubled months they had co-ordinated their varied skills and giftings to work with both Leslie and Eddie. At times they had been at their wit's end as Eddie would seem to make progress and then fall back into his old way of thinking and reacting. At such times they almost despaired of bringing about any long-term healing or change. Yet perhaps the fact that they were working as a team helped them not to give up, but to trust God for the outcome and for his timing. After all, wasn't Eddie basically the Lord's problem?

One of the ways Eddie needed to change was in being willing to take responsibility - something which he'd never bothered about in the past. But now he wanted to show Leslie that he was willing and able to hold down a job and he found employment in a joiner's shop until he was paid off just before Christmas. Next he found night work cleaning helicopters and at the same time he worked as a part-time hospital cleaner during the day. Surely Leslie would be convinced of his sincerity if he managed to do two *jobs*?

Shortly afterwards they decided to move from the flat and try to buy a house instead. Eddie guessed it wouldn't be easy when he didn't have a proper full-time job, but they prayed as they house hunted and the Lord led them to a house in Donview Road, Aberdeen, and also enabled them to get a mortgage.

Almost at once Eddie got full-time employment with British Rail. Reading Psalm One that day, Eddie was overwhelmed by all the Lord was doing for them. 'All that he does prospers,' he read at the end of verse three. Would the Lord continue to make that happen for him? he wondered.

The subsequent months and promotion examinations have confirmed to Eddie that the Lord is indeed with him. He is now a leading trackman with British Rail, while Leslie continues her work at the YMCA. They both worship at the Abbey Fellowship, the first place in Aberdeen where Eddie had found positive help when he came out of prison.

Eddie has not forgotten his time in prison. He has even been back inside! Not for any crime but both he and Leslie are members of the Prison Fellowship group which meets once a month in Aberdeen to pray for prisoners and then goes into Craiginches Prison to hold meetings and talk to the men there, in the hope that they too can find Jesus, or be built up in their faith. Eddie also writes to some of the men and sends in Christian books.

He has revisited Glenochil Prison where he spoke about his experiences, both in jail and on the 'outside'. Occasionally he is asked to tell his story in churches or at young people's meetings where his stocky, physical presence gives credence to the tales he tells about his violent past, while his friendly, open countenance is clear evidence of what the Lord has done, and is still doing, in this man's life.

Centuries ago, through the prophet Isaiah, the Lord said of Jesus that he would not break the bruised reed. As Eddie has given Jesus control of his life in all its detail, so Jesus is keeping his promise to heal the effects of the early bruising which Eddie suffered as a child, and enabled him to grow to full stature in Christ. The once bruised reed is beginning to stand tall. He knows that healing is an ongoing process and that there will still be battles ahead. But his confidence is no longer in himself and his own strength - these have let him down too often in the past!

Together in Christ, Eddie and Leslie look forward to whatever the future holds, knowing that 'he who calls them is faithful'.

At the time of writing Eddie was again preparing for parenthood. Eddie and Leslie were delighted to receive the gift of a baby daughter, Fiona, on 13 May 1993.

A FINAL WORD

from Douglas McIntyre,
Pastor of Abbey Christian Fellowship

On reading this book you may conclude that both myself and the Wendes were the only contributors to Eddie and Leslie's situation. In fact the whole church was involved.

Fundamental to any counselling process is prayer. One of the main difficulties that we face with any problem is that, while everyone appreciates the value of prayer, they are often reluctant to inform others of their difficulties.

Very few people within the church knew the specifics of Eddie and Leslie's situation, but the vast majority knew that there was some difficulty that needed to be prayed into. This level of involvement in prayer is something that everyone can share in. No special qualifications or eloquence are needed. If you know the Lord and that he is the answer to every problem, then you are qualified.

There is no doubt that counsellors and psychologists can help many folk with a variety of problems, but from experience we know that there is a work that only the Holy Spirit can perform within an

individual. The Holy Spirit is not in the business of
helping us to merely cope with life's problems, he is
in the business of converting, transforming - changing old into new.

The work of the Holy Spirit is released through
prayer and received into our lives through a willingness to submit to the will of God. We need to
recognise that God's will is not something to be
feared, but to be welcomed as the best plan.

In his letter to the Romans Paul states that the
Holy Spirit helps us in our weakness. Many of us
have grown up with the understanding that failure is
not tolerated by God and therefore cuts us off from
him. Quite the reverse is true. In times of weakness,
he doesn't abandon us, in fact he draws alongside us.
His love for us begins to minister to our hearts,
healing the wounds and removing from us the obsta-
cles that would try to hinder our progress.

The Holy Spirit is presented to us as a Counsellor,
the one who comforts and strengthens. Our prayers
are to invite him into the centre of any difficulty that
we might face. The Abbey's starting point in this
story was to pray.

Through prayer, love and support are released. It
is difficult to pray without being moved by a desire
to help. While the focus of our problem solving is on
counselling, I believe that counselling can be very
clinical and often hollow, unless we have the support
and love of a community of people who are willing
to draw near. It would be difficult to number the

many people who gave of their time in so many different ways - people who responded to pleas for help often regardless of the time of day or night and regardless of personal inconvenience.

The following points are based on our experience and the lessons we learned. As I have already mentioned, prayer and the involvement of the Holy Spirit are vital. The church must see its role as a caring community, not through the efforts of its paid professionals, but through its functioning as the Body of Christ. Everyone is uniquely gifted and therefore able to make a valuable contribution.

Discernment is another important ingredient - knowing exactly what we are dealing with; avoiding being conned or misled while remaining true to the central focus of the real problem.

Prejudice is also to be avoided. It is so easy to pre-judge people who are different or whose problems fall outwith one's own experience. We must consider - is it to Christ that we are asking people to conform, or to our understanding of middle-class Christianity? We must not consider ourselves better, because we are all sinners, born with the same capacity for sin.

Love conquers all. For the most part, Eddie struggled to trust because he grew up in an environment where to trust could get you killed. As a result he didn't trust anyone. Winning Eddie's trust was an important first step. Once he had confided his problems, Eddie was often insecure, wondering whether he had done the right thing. His behaviour at times was difficult to cope with, but hanging in tough is often what is needed. Remember that God hangs in tough for us.

Loving the unlovely does not come naturally. People who are different are perceived as being unlovely. Our rejection of them will only deepen the hole in which they find themselves. In fact, through their actions and speech they will often invite rejection. The love of Christ in us needs to help us rise above our base instincts which tell us that we don't need the hassle.

We don't have all the answers. Pride will often cloud our judgment. We will feel the need to complete the task on our own. If we are acting in the best interests of the individual, we will conclude that there are specialists outside our immediate circle who could provide valuable input. Their expertise may be another piece of the jigsaw. In Eddie's situation we involved outside agencies and worked with them where we felt it was appropriate.

Being willing to confront and take a clear stand on issues requires courage at the best of times, but it requires an even greater level of courage when one is confronted with threats of violence. A satisfactory outcome will never be achieved if we fudge issues. It takes two to make a marriage and two to break it. Taking sides is not our role. A balanced perspective is needed - an ability to help the individual to see their fault and to rise from the ashes of being a victim to take some responsibility for change in their life. Tough decisions are never easy to make or implement.

But with God nothing is impossible. No situation is beyond hope. In Jesus there is an answer to every situation. Eddie and Leslie are testimony to the grace and power of God. What often seemed hopeless, lost in a sea of insurmountable problems, when touched by the Lord, changed. Be strong and never give up. Help is on the way.

Some of you reading this book may be surprised at the time scale. Eddie and Leslie's situation did not change quickly, overnight. The need to persevere is great. We need to give things time to change little by little. Problems that have taken a lifetime to grow and flourish will not always be quickly removed. Our pride and victim-based perspective often hinder the process, but the Lord is patient and we must be patient too.

So, what did the Abbey do? We endeavoured to love, to be accessible and available, to be faithful to the prompting of the Holy Spirit. But to be honest it was a case of ordinary people serving an extraordinary God.

I need to thank the many people who were willing to get involved, who gave of their time freely and were willing to be a clear manifestation of the Father's love.

Needless to say this story has not ended. Eddie and Leslie are continuing to work things out. They have taken great steps forward and there is a real sense in which the back of their problems has been broken. Eddie continues to have a desire to serve the Lord in ministry and to share his testimony widely.

AND YOU VISITED ME

The Story of Prison Fellowship Scotland
edited by Betty McKay and Louise Purvis

ISBN 1-85792-005-8   192 pages

In 1981 when Louise Purvis organised the first meeting of Prison Fellowship in Scotland, she little knew what she was taking on. As secretary and then coordinator of the work of visitation in 18 penal institutions, it became virtually a fulltime job. Taking probationers and remand prisoners into her own home was a further example of a commitment which went beyond duty. The work has grown since these small beginnings, with over thirty support groups and a fulltime director.

Now you can read about the results of that work - stories of ex-inmates, prison visitors, warders and some 'lifers'. The common bond they have is that their lives have been touched by God. His power to transform people is clearly seen in these personal and searching testimonies.

Chuck Colson in his foreword writes, 'The Spirit's inexorable power is not confined to compelling individual men and women; he also calls into being powerful movements throughout history .... Nowhere is this more evident than in Prison Fellowship Scotland.'

If any reader wishes to contact Eddie
Murison then please send for details to
Christian Focus Publications Ltd
Geanies House, Fearn, Ross-shire,
IV20 1TW, Scotland, Great Britain.